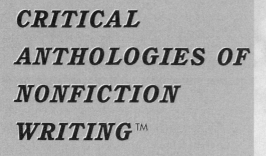

CRITICAL ANTHOLOGIES OF NONFICTION WRITING™

CRITICAL PERSPECTIVES ON CLIMATE DISRUPTION

Edited by
Robert Chehoski

THE ROSEN PUBLISHING GROUP, INC.
NEW YORK

For young conservationists, environmentalists, scientists, naturalists, politicians, and great thinkers. Together, you can help create tomorrow's solutions for a healthier planet.

Published in 2006 by The Rosen Publishing Group, Inc.
29 East 21st Street, New York, NY 10010

Library of Congress Cataloging-in-Publication Data

Critical perspectives on climate disruption/edited by Robert Chehoski.—1st ed.
 p. cm.—(Critical anthologies of nonfiction writing)
Includes bibliographical references and index.
ISBN 1-4042-0539-X (library binding)
1. Climatic changes—Environmental aspects. 2. Global warming.
I. Chehoski, Robert. II. Series.
QC981.8.C5C77 2006
363.738'74—dc22

                                        2005015779

On the cover: Paul Hardy photographed this chemical plant in Scotland, United Kingdom, in 2001.

CONTENTS

INTRODUCTION

o matter how compelling the controversy surrounding climate change and its relationship to global warming may appear to be, there is now substantial scientific evidence to verify their connection. Consider, for example, the scientific reports published by the 800 scientists who make up the Intergovernmental Panel on Climate Change (IPCC). It is the consensus of most of the world's top scientific associations and organizations that Earth has already warmed enough to alter global climate dramatically. In fact, IPCC chairman Dr. Rajendra Pachauri warned scientists from 114 nations at an international conference in January 2005. As reported in *World Affairs: The Issues Journal of Scientific Climate*, Pachauri stated, "Climate change is for real. We have just a small window of opportunity and it is closing rather rapidly. There is not a moment to lose. We are risking the ability of the human race to survive." Calculations now estimate that the average temperature of Earth will increase as much as 4 to 10 degrees Fahrenheit (2.2 to 5.6 degrees Celsius) over the next century, in part because of human-driven industrial pollution. This increase will ultimately be cataclysmic if policies and systems are not established to counteract the inevitable changes, particularly in developing countries.

Even without reading the overwhelming data on the subject, we know of regions that have already been experiencing the effects of global warming. In the Arctic, for instance, glaciers are melting at an alarming rate. The actual weather patterns in the region are changing, too, and temperatures there are climbing about nine times faster than anywhere else on Earth, according to Robert W. Corell, a senior fellow with the American Meteorological Society and chairman of the Arctic Climate Impact Assessment Group. The Arctic's Inuit population, already reeling from changes in temperature, is concerned about rising sea levels that are increasingly swollen by water from melting glaciers and ice sheets. In other instances, melting permafrost in western Siberia has the potential to unleash millions of tons of methane—an extremely potent greenhouse gas—into the atmosphere. Sergei Kirpotin, a botanist at Tomsk State University in Russia, described the conditions in Siberia as an "ecological landslide that is probably irreversible" in an August 2005 issue of *New Scientist*.

In Europe, climate changes are nearly as severe. In 2003, the deaths of 35,000 people, many of them elderly residents without air conditioning, have since been attributed to the unprecedented summer heat waves throughout Europe in that year. In northern Europe, some ski resorts have been forced to use snow machines as a result of rising temperatures, while others have closed their doors entirely. In other examples, scientists have relocated dozens of species of plants and animals to northern regions so that they can reestablish themselves before rising temperatures in their traditional environments cause their extinction.

In the United States, the changes are far subtler. Some scientists have linked the rise in powerful hurricanes to warmer ocean temperatures. Warmer temperatures have also increased the breeding habitats for insects such as mosquitoes, paving the way for an increased incidence of West Nile virus, which has now spread to nearly all of the United States. Many doctors have also seen a marked increase in asthma, which they attribute to global warming. (In May 2004, the *Lancet* reported a 160 percent increase in asthma among preschool children between 1980 and 1994.) Observers around the country have pointed to other markers, too, such as the early migration of birds and the early development of spring blossoms.

Even as the evidence that substantiates global warming mounts around the world, some people maintain that the increasing temperatures are normal fluctuations in weather patterns or part of a change in Earth's solar cycle. In many cases, environmentalists attempting to increase awareness of the subject of climate change are silenced or condemned as zealots who are attempting to politicize science. Even best-selling author Michael Crichton, whose recent novel *State of Fear* is about a band of rebel ecoterrorists engineering catastrophic weather disruptions, is contributing to the blurred line between fantasy and reality.

Crichton, who in January 2005 took the stage at an event for members of the American Enterprise Institute (AEI), condemned recent scientific findings about global warming as "shockingly flawed and unsubstantiated." Unfortunately, an increasing number of conservative think tanks also support these views. More and more, however, reporters around the country are finding that many of these so-called conservative think tanks are heavily funded by big business. An exposé in the May/June 2005 issue of *Mother Jones*, for example, found that Exxon/Mobil had funneled more than $8 million into forty such groups between 2000 and 2003. According to Ross Gelbspan, the goal of these conservative organizations is to influence public policy. According to Gelbspan, they want to curtail laws that may be created to limit pollution and carbon emissions.Gelbspan claims that conservative groups want to keep Americans misinformed or blur the line between the moneymaking interests of the private sector and the more ethical interests of lawmakers. He thinks that big business has helped keep Americans skeptical about the reality of global warming and the immediate need to act. American corporations have influenced many Americans into believing that global warming is not a threat to humanity.

In keeping with this ambivalence, the Bush administration has decided to back out of the 1997 Kyoto Protocol, an agreement signed between 141 nations in February 2005 that hopes to reduce carbon emissions by 5 percent over the next century. International scientists associated with the IPCC say this isn't enough; they claim that global emissions need to be reduced by 50 to 70 percent in order to make any significant difference in future warming trends. Still, the Bush administration's reluctance has sent a message of hubris to other nations, a decision that placed the needs of the U.S. economy over the needs of the entire world. Critics of the United States add that global warming will have its greatest and most immediate impact in developing nations around the world.

To counteract this trend, many U.S. states have begun to voluntarily initiate their own pollution-control measures. According to Massachusetts Institute of Technology (MIT) professor Mario J. Molina, this is an important first step.

Molina, who recently gave a lecture on air quality and climate change in Bangkok, was one of a group of scientists who won a Nobel Prize in Chemistry in 1995 for drawing attention to the threat posed to the ozone layer from chlorofluorocarbon (CFC) gases. As a result of Molina's work, these gases, once used as propellants in spray cans and as refrigerants and solvents, have now been mostly eliminated. Molina says, "Society must help in saving the planet. [Global warming] is no longer [just] a science issue, but a social issue."

For today's students, who may be among the first generation to see the direct implications of rising temperatures as well as the exhaustion of Earth's fossil fuels, an understanding of how climate change will affect our society has never been more important. Today's students can make an immediate effort to conserve energy and fuel, reduce greenhouse gases and pollution, and lead the fight to a cleaner, more fuel-efficient country and world.

CHAPTER ONE

TIME, CONTINUITY, AND CHANGE: THE EVOLUTION OF CLIMATE CHANGE

Ross Gelbspan, one of the nation's leading writers on issues related to climate change and its effects, was among the first authors to closely examine issues surrounding global warming. This particular piece, an essay that appeared in Harper's *magazine in December 1995, drew national attention to weather events in the early to mid-1990s, including heat waves, floods, and droughts that were believed to have been linked to global warming. Gelbspan, who has since devoted his career to educating the public on the issues surrounding climate change and the creation of policies related to global warming, was a finalist for a national magazine award for this early article on the effects of rising temperatures. —RC*

From "The Heat Is On"
by Ross Gelbspan
Harper's, December 1995

After my lawn had burned away to straw last summer, and the local papers announced that the season had been one of the driest in recorded history of New England, I found myself wondering how long we can go on pretending that nothing is amiss with the world's weather. It wasn't just the fifty ducks near my house that had died when falling water levels in a creek exposed them to botulism-infested mud, or the five hundred people dead in the Midwest from an unexpected heat wave that followed the season's second "one-hundred-year flood" in three years. It was also the news from New Orleans (overrun by an extraordinary number of cockroaches and termites after a fifth consecutive winter without a killing frost), from Spain (suffering a fourth year of drought in a region that ordinarily enjoys a rainfall of 84 inches a year), and from London (Britain's meteorological office reporting the driest summer since 1727 and the hottest since 1659).

The reports of changes in the world's climate have been with us for fifteen or twenty years, most urgently since 1988, when Dr. James Hansen, director of NASA's Goddard Institute for Space Studies, declared that the era of global warming was at hand. As a newspaper correspondent who had reported on the United Nations Conferences on the environment in Stockholm in 1972 and in Rio in 1992, I understood something of the ill effects apt to result from the extravagant burning of oil and coal. New record-setting weather extremes seem to have become as commonplace as traffic accidents, and three simple facts have long been known: the distance from the surface of the earth to the far edge of the inner atmosphere is only twelve miles; the annual amount of carbon dioxide forced into that limited space is six billion tons; and the ten hottest years in recorded human history have all occurred since 1980. The facts beg a question that is as simple to ask as it is hard to answer. What do we do with what we know?

The question became more pointed in September, when the 2,500 climate scientists serving on the Intergovernmental Panel on Climate Change issued a new statement on the prospect of forthcoming catastrophe. Never before had the IPCC (called into existence in 1988) come to so unambiguous a conclusion. Always in years past there had been people saying that we didn't yet know enough, or that the evidence was problematic, or our system of computer simulation was subject to too many uncertainties. Not this year. The panel flatly announced that the earth had entered a period of Climactic instability likely to cause "widespread economic, social and environmental dislocation over the next century." The continuing emission of greenhouse gases would create protracted, crop-destroying droughts in continental interiors, a host of new and recurring diseases, hurricanes of extraordinary malevolence, and rising sea levels that could inundate island nations and low-lying coastal rims on the continents.

I came across the report in the *New York Times* during the same week that the island of St. Thomas was blasted to shambles by one of thirteen hurricanes that roiled the Caribbean this fall. Scientists speak the language of probability. They prefer to avoid making statements that cannot be further corrected, reinterpreted, modified, or proven wrong. If its September announcement was uncharacteristically bold, possibly it was because the IPCC scientists understood that they were addressing their remarks to people profoundly unwilling to hear what they had to say.

That resistance is understandable, given the immensity of the stakes. The energy industries now constitute the largest single enterprise known to mankind. Moreover, they are indivisible from automotive, farming, shipping, air freight, and banking interests, as well as from the governments dependent on oil revenues for their very existence. With annual sales in excess of one trillion dollars and daily sales of more than two billion dollars, the oil industry alone supports the economies of the Middle East and large segments of the economies of Russia, Mexico, Venezuela, Nigeria, Indonesia, Norway, and Great Britain. Begin to enforce restriction on the consumption of oil and coal, and the effects on the global economy—unemployment, depression, social breakdown, and war—might lay waste to what we have come to call civilization. It is no wonder that for the last five or six years many of the world's politicians and most of the world's news media have been promoting the perception that the worries about the weather are overwrought. Ever since the IPCC first set out to devise strategies whereby the nations of the world might reduce their carbon dioxide emissions, and thus ward off a rise in the average global temperature on the order of 4 or 5 degrees Celsius (roughly equal in magnitude to the difference between the last ice age and the current Climactic period), the energy industry has been conducting, not unreasonably, a ferocious public relations campaign meant to sell the notion that science, any science, is always a matter of uncertainty. Yet on reading the news from the IPCC, I wondered how the oil company publicists would confront the most recent series of geophysical events and scientific findings. To wit:

> •A 48-by-22 miles chunk of the Larsen Ice Shelf
> in the Antarctic broke off last March, exposing
> rocks that had been buried for 20,000 years
> and prompting Rodolfo del Valle of the

Argentine Antarctic Institute to tell the Associated Press, "Last November we predicted the [ice shelf] would crack in ten years, but it has happened in barely two months."

• In April, researchers discovered a 70 percent decline in the population of zooplankton off the coast of southern California, raising questions about the survival of several species of fish that feed on it. Scientists have linked the change to a 1 to 2 degree C increase in the surface water temperature over the last four decades.

• A recent series of articles in *The Lancet*, a British medical journal, linked changes in climate patterns to the spread of infectious diseases around the world. The *Aedes aegypti* mosquito, which spreads dengue fever and yellow fever, has traditionally been unable to survive the altitudes higher than 1,000 meters above sea level. But these mosquitoes are now being reported at 1,150 meters in Costa Rica and at 2,200 meters in Colombia. Ocean warming has triggered algae blooms linked to outbreaks of cholera in India, Bangladesh, and the Pacific coast of South America, where, in 1991, the disease infected more than 400,000 people.

• In a paper published in *Science* in April, David J. Thomson, of the AT&T Bell Laboratories, concluded that the 0.6 degree C warning of the average global temperature over the past century correlates directly with the buildup of atmospheric carbon dioxide. Separate findings by a team of scientists at the National Oceanic and Atmospheric Administration's National Climactic Data Center indicate that growing weather extremes in the United States are due, by a probability of 90 percent, to rising levels of greenhouse gases.

• Scientists previously believed that the transitions between ice ages and more moderate climate periods occur gradually, over centuries. But researchers from the Woods Hole Oceanographic Institution, examining deep ocean sediment and ice core samples, found that these shifts, with their temperature changes of up to 7 degrees C, have occurred within three to four decades—a virtual nanosecond in geological time. Over the last 70,000 years, the earth's climate has snapped into radically different temperature regimes. "Our results suggest that the present climate system is very delicately poised," said researcher Scott Lehman. "Shifts could happen very rapidly if conditions are right, and we cannot predict when that will occur." His cautionary tone is underscored by findings that the end of the last ice age, some 8,000 years ago, was preceded by a series of extreme oscillations in which severe regional deep freezes alternated with warming spikes. As

the North Atlantic warmed, Arctic snowmelts
and increased rainfall diluted the salt content
of the ocean, which, in turn, redirected the
ocean's warming current from a northeasterly
direction to one that ran nearly due east. Should
such an episode occur today, say researchers,
"the present climate of Britain and Norway
would change suddenly to that of Greenland."

These items (and many like them) would seem to be alarming
news—far more important than the candidacy of Colin
Powell, or even whether Newt Gingrich believes the government should feed poor children—worthy of a national debate
or the sustained attention of Congress. But the signs and portents have been largely ignored, relegated to the
environmental press and the oddball margins of the mass
media. More often than not, the news about the accelerating
retreat of the world's glaciers or the heat- and insect-stressed
Canadian forests comes qualified with the observation that
the question of global warming never can be conclusively
resolved. The confusion is intentional, expensively gift
wrapped by the energy industries.

Capital keeps its nose to the wind. The people who run the
world's oil and coal companies know that the march of science,
and the political action, may be slowed by disinformation. In the
last year and a half, one of the leading oil industry public relations outlets, the Global Climate Coalition, has spent more than
a million dollars to downplay the threat of climate change. It
expects to spend another $850,000 on the issue next year.
Similarly, the National Coal Association spent more than

$700,000 on the global climate issue in 1992 and 1993. In 1993 alone, the American Petroleum Institute, just one of fifty-four industry members of the GCC, paid $1.8 million to the public relations firm of Burson-Marsteller partly in an effort to defeat a proposed tax on fossil fuels. For perspective, this is only slightly less than the combined yearly expenditures on global warming of the five major environmental groups that focus on climate issues—about $2.1 million, according to the officials of the Environmental Defense Fund, the Natural Resources Defense Council, the Sierra Club, the Union of Concerned Scientists, and the World Wildlife Fund.

For the most part the industry has relied on a small band of skeptics—Dr. Richard S. Lindzen, Dr. Pat Michaels, Dr. Robert Balling, Dr. Sjerwood Idso, and Dr. S. Fred Singer, among others—who have proven extraordinarily adept at draining the issue of all sense of crisis. Through their frequent pronouncements in the press and on the radio and television, they have helped create the illusion that the question is hopelessly mired in unknowns. Most damaging has been their influence on decision makers; their contrarian views have allowed conservative Republicans such as Representative Dana Rohrabacher (R., Calif.) to dismiss legitimate research concerns as "liberal claptrap" and have provided the basis for the recent round of budget cuts to those government science programs designed to monitor the health of the planet.

Last May, Minnesota held hearings in St. Paul to determine the environmental cost of coal burning by state power plants. Three of the skeptics—Lindzen, Michaels, and Balling—were hired as expert witnesses to testify on behalf of

Western Fuel Association, a $400 million consortium of coal suppliers and coal-fired utilities.[1]

An especially aggressive industry player, Western Fuels was quite candid about its strategy in two annual reports:

> [T]here has been a close to universal impulse in the trade association community here in Washington to concede the scientific premise of global warming . . . while arguing over policy prescriptions that would be the least disruptive to our economy . . . We have disagreed, and do disagree, with this strategy. When [the climate change] controversy first erupted . . . scientists were found who are skeptical about much of what seemed generally accepted about the potential for climate change.

Among them were Michaels, Balling, and S. Fred Singer.

Lindzen, a distinguished professor of meteorology at MIT, testified in St. Paul that the maximum probable warming of the atmosphere in the face of a doubling of carbon dioxide emissions over the next century would amount to no more than a negligible 0.3 degrees C. Michaels, who teaches climatology at the University of Virginia, stated that he foresaw no increase in the rate of sea level rise—another feared precursor of global warming. Balling, who works on climate issues at Arizona State University, declared that the increase in emissions would boost the average global temperature by no more than one degree.

At first glance, these attacks appear defensible, given their focus on the black holes of uncertainty that mark our current knowledge of the planet's exquisitely interrelated climate system. The skeptics emphasize the inadequacy of a major climate research tool known as a General Circulation Model, and our ignorance of carbon dioxide exchanges between the oceans and the atmosphere and of the various roles of clouds. They have repeatedly pointed out that although the world's output of carbon dioxide has exploded since 1940, there has been no corresponding increase in the global temperature. The larger scientific community, by contrast, holds that this is due to the masking effect on the earth, and to a time lag in the ocean's absorption and release of carbon dioxide.

But while the skeptics portray themselves as besieged truth-seekers fending off irresponsible environmental doomsayers, their testimony in St. Paul and elsewhere revealed the source and scope of their funding for the first time. Michaels has received more than $115,000 over the last four years from coal and energy interests. *World Climate Review*, a quarterly he founded that routinely debunks climate concerns, was funded by Western Fuels. Over the last six years, either alone or with colleagues, Balling has received more than $200,000 from coal and oil interests in Great Britain, Germany, and elsewhere. Balling (along with Sherwood Idso) has also taken money from Cyprus Minerals, a mining company that has been a major funder of People for the West—a militantly anti-environmental "Wise Use" group. Lindzen, for his part, charges oil and coal interests $2,500 a day for his consulting services; his 1991 trip to testify before a Senate committee was paid for by Western Fuels, and a speech he wrote, entitled "Global Warming: the Origin and Nature of Alleged Scientific Consensus," was underwritten by OPEC. Singer, who last winter proposed a $95,000 publicity project to "stem the tide towards ever more onerous controls on energy use," has received consulting fees from Exxon, Shell, Unocal, ARCO, and Sun Oil, and has warned them that they face the same threat as the chemical firms that produced chlorofluorocarbons (CFCs), a class of chemicals found to be depleting atmospheric ozone. "It took only five years to go from . . . a simple freeze of production [of CFCs]," Singer has written, " . . . to the 1992 decision of a complete production phase-out—all on the basis of quite insubstantial science."[2]

The skeptics assert flatly that their science is untainted by funding. Nevertheless, in the persistent and well-funded campaign of denial they have become interchangeable ornaments on the hood of a high-powered engine of disinformation. Their dissenting opinions are amplified beyond all proportion through the media while the concerns of the dominant majority of the world's scientific establishment are marginalized.[3] By keeping the discussion focused on whether there is a problem in the first place, they have effectively silenced the debate over what to do about it.

Last spring's IPCC conference in Berlin is a good example. Delegations from 170 nations met to negotiate targets and timetable for the reducing the world's carbon dioxide emissions. The efforts of the conference ultimately foundered on foot-dragging by the United States and Japan and active resistance from the OPEC nations. Leading the fight for the most dramatic reduction—to 60 percent of 1990 levels—was a coalition of small island nations from the Caribbean and the Pacific that fear being flooded out of existence. They were supported by the most western European governments, but China and India, with their vast coal resources, argued that until the

United States significantly cuts its own emissions, their obligation to develop their own economies outranked their obligation to the global environment. In the end, OPEC, supported by the United States, Japan, Australia, Canada, New Zealand, rejected calls to limit emissions, declaring emission limits premature.

As the natural crisis escalates, so will the forces of institutional and societal denial. If, at the cost of corporate pocket change, industrial giants can control the publicly perceived reality of the condition of the planet and the state of our scientific knowledge, what would they do if their survival were truly put at risk? Billions would be spent on the creation of information and the control of politicians. Glad-handing oil company ads on the op-ed page of the *New York Times* (from a quarter-page pronouncement by Mobil last September 28: "There's a lot of good news out there") would give way to a new stream of selective findings by privatized scientists. Long before the planet itself collapsed, democracy would break apart under the stress of "natural" disasters. It is not difficult to foresee that in an ecological state of emergency our political liberties would be the first casualties.

Thus, the question must be asked: can civilization change the way it operates? For 5,000 years, we have thought of ourselves as dependent children of the earth, flourishing or perishing according to the whims of nature. But with the explosion of the power of our technology and the size of our population, our activities have grown to the proportion of geological forces, affecting the major systems of the planet. Short of the Atlantic washing away half of Florida, the abstract notion that the old anomalies have become the new norm is difficult to grasp. Dr. James McCarthy of Harvard who has supervised the work of climate scientists from sixty nations, puts it this way: "If the last 150 years had been marked by the kind of climate instability we are now seeing, the world would never have been able to support its present population of 5 billion people." We live in a world of man-sized urgencies, measured in hours or days. What unfolds slowly is not, by our lights, urgent, and it will therefore take a collective act of imagination to understand the extremity of the situation we now confront. The lag time in our planet's ecological systems will undoubtedly delay these decisions, and even if the nations of the world were to agree tomorrow on a plan to phase out oil and coal and convert to renewable energies, an equivalent lag time in human affairs would delay its implementation for years. What too many people refuse to understand is that the global economy's existence depends upon the global environment, not the other way around. One cannot negotiate jobs, development, or rates of economic growth without nature.

What of the standard list of palliatives—carbon taxes, more energy-efficient buildings, a revival of public transportation? The ideas are attractive, but the thinking is too small. Even were the United States to halve its own carbon dioxide contribution, this cutback would soon be overwhelmed by the coming development of industry and housing and schools in China and India and Mexico for their billions of citizens. No solution can work that does not provide ample energy resources for the development of the world's nations.

So here is an informal proposal—at best a starting point for a conversation—from one man who is not an expert. What if we turned the deserts of the world into electricity farms? Let the Middle East countries keep their oil royalties as solar royalties. What if the world mobilized around a ten-year project to phase out all fossil fuels, to develop renewable energy technologies, to extend those technologies to every corner of the world? What if, to minimize the conflict of so massive a dislocation, the world's energy companies were put in charge of the transition—answering only to an international regulatory body and an enforceable timetable? Grant them the same profit margins for solar electricity and hydrogen fuel they now receive from petroleum and coal. Give them the licenses for all renewable energy technologies. Assure them the same relative position in the world's economy they now enjoy at the end of the project.

Are these ideas mere dreams? Perhaps, but there are historical reasons to have hope. Four years ago a significant fraction of humanity overturned its Communist system in a historical blink of an eye. Eight years ago the world's governments joined together in Montreal to regulate CFCs. Technology is not the issue. The atomic bomb was developed in two and a half years. Putting a man on the moon took eleven. Surely, given the same sense of urgency, we can develop new energy systems in ten years. Most of the technology is already available to us or soon will be. We have the knowledge, the energy, and the hunger for jobs to get it done. And we are different in one unmeasurable way from previous generations: ours is the first to be educated about the larger world by the global reach of electronic information.

The leaders of the oil and coal industry, along with their skeptical scientists, relentlessly accuse environmentalists of overstating the Climactic threat to destroy capitalism. Must a transformation that is merely technological dislodge the keystone of economic order? I don't know. But I do know that technology changes the way we conceive the world. To transform our economy would oblige us to understand the limits of the planet. That understanding alone might seed the culture with a more organic concept of ourselves and our connectedness to the earth. And corporations, it is useful to remember, are not only obstacles on the road to the future. They are also crucibles of technology and organizing engines of production, the modern expression of mankind's drive for creativity. The industrialist is no less human than the poet, and both the climate scientist and the oil company operator inhabit the same planet, suffer the same short life span, harbor the same hopes for their children.

Each summer, our family walks the deep north Maine woods in search of adventure and a sense of renewal. The trip this year was different for me; I was visited by premonitions of the coming sickness of the forests, haunted by unwelcome and indescribably sad imaginings. They intruded at unexpected moments. One night while listening to a dialog of loons on the black lake I suddenly experienced a momentary feeling of bottomless grief. Struck by the recognition of how fragile was the frame of the world, and how easily it could be shattered by our mutual distrust and confusion, I feared that the cause of survival would be lost to the greed and alienation and shortsightedness that dog our few last steps to the threshold of the millennium. My dream of reconfiguring the global economy was probably nothing more than the hopeless longing of a reporter, not a social thinker or macroeconomic engineer.

But I am also a husband, a father, a son, and a grandson. And someday perhaps a grandfather. Our history is rich with visionaries urging us to change our way of thinking, asking questions about the meaning of the past and the shape of the future. Now the questions are being posed, in a language we don't yet fully understand, by the oceans. I have promised myself that next summer I will keep my lawn watered, at least as long as the water holds out.

Source Notes

1. In 1991, Western Fuels spent an estimated $250,000 to produce and distribute a video entitled "The Greening of Planet Earth," which was shown frequently inside the Bush White House as well as within the governments of OPEC. In near-evangelical tones, the video promises that a new age of agricultural abundance will result from increasing concentrations of carbon dioxide–forced growth of new grasslands where the earth's diminishing forests are replenished by a nurturing atmosphere. Unfortunately, it overlooks the bugs. Experts note that even a minor elevation in temperature would trigger an explosion in the planet's insect population, leading to potentially significant disruptions in food supplies from crop damage as well as to a surge of insect-borne diseases. It appears that Western Fuels' video fails to tell people what the termites in New Orleans may be trying to tell them now.

2. Contrary to his assertion, however, virtually all relevant researchers say the link between CFCs and ozone depletion is based on unassailably solid scientific evidence. As if to underscore the point, in May the research director of the European Union Commission estimated that last winter's ozone loss will result in about 80,000 additional cases of skin cancer in Europe. This fall, the three scientists who discovered the CFC-ozone link won the Nobel Prize for Chemistry.

3. The industry's public relations arsenal, however, is made up of much more than a few sympathetic scientists. Last March, the Global Climate Coalition distributed a report by Accu-Weather Inc. that denied any significant increase in extreme weather events. The report flies in the face of contradictory evidence cited by officials of the insurance industry, which, during the 1980s, paid an average of $3 billion a year to victims of natural disasters—a figure that has jumped to $10 billion a year in this decade. A top official of a Swiss reinsurance firm told the World Watch Institute: "There is a significant body of scientific evidence indicating that [the recent] record insured loss from natural catastrophes was not a random occurrence." More succinctly, the president of the Reinsurance Association of America said climate change "could bankrupt the industry."

*While little argument can be presented to challenge the existence
of climate change resulting from global warming, uncertainty
about predicting the rate of this change continues to be a subject
of debate among the world's scientists. John Houghton,
cochair of the Intergovernmental Panel on Climate Change
(IPCC), says, "The rate of warming is far greater than it has
been for the past 10,000 years." This leads researchers to
conclude that the recent dramatic rise in temperatures is not
due to a natural shift in climate. In this excerpt from his book*
Global Warming: The Complete Briefing, *Houghton
explains the science behind his conclusion in clear language
that can be embraced by scientists and students alike. He
explains the science behind the greenhouse effect and some of
the natural variables, such as El Niño events or volcanic eruptions, that can also alter temperatures. —RC*

From *Global Warming: The Complete Briefing*
by John Houghton
1994

Before studying future climate changes, what can be said
about climate change in the past? In the more distant past
there have been very large changes. The last million years
have seen a succession of major ice ages interspersed with
warmer periods. The last of these ice ages began to come to
an end about 20,000 years ago and we are now in what is
called an interglacial period . . . But have there been changes
in the very much shorter period of living memory—over the
past few decades?

Variations in the day-to-day weather are occurring all the time; they are very much part of our lives. The climate of a region is its average weather over a period which may be a few months, a season or a few years . . . In the British Isles, as in many parts of the world, no season is the same as the last or indeed the same as any previous season, nor will it be repeated in detail next time round. Most of these variations we take for granted; they add a lot of interest to our lives. Those we particularly notice are the extreme situations and the climate disasters. Most of the worst disasters in the world are, in fact, weather- or climate-related . . .

The 1980s: A Remarkable Decade

The 1980s were unusually warm. Globally speaking, the decade has been the warmest since accurate records began somewhat over a hundred years ago and unusually warm years have continued into the 1990s. In terms of global average near surface air temperature, the year 1995 was the warmest on record and eight of the nine warmest years in the record occurred in the 1980s and early 1990s.

The period has also been remarkable (just how remarkable will be considered later) for the frequency and intensity of extremes of weather and climate. For example, periods of unusually strong winds have been experienced in western Europe. During the early hours of the morning of 16 October 1987, over fifteen million trees were blown down in southeast England and the London area. The storm also hit Northern France, Belgium and Holland with ferocious intensity; it turned out to be the worst storm experienced in the area since 1703. Storm-force winds of similar intensity but covering a greater area of western Europe struck on several occasions in January and February 1990.

But those storms in Europe were mild by comparison with the much more intense and damaging storms other parts of the world have experienced during these years. About eighty hurricanes and typhoons—other names for tropical cyclones—occur around the tropical oceans each year, familiar enough to be given names. Hurricane Gilbert, which caused devastation on the island of Jamaica and the coast of Mexico in 1988, and Hurricane Andrew, which caused a great deal of damage in Florida and other regions of the southern United States in 1992, have been notable recent examples. Low-lying areas such as Bangladesh are particularly vulnerable to the storm surges associated with tropical cyclones; the combined effect of intensely low atmospheric pressure, extremely strong winds and high tides causes a surge of water which can reach far inland. In one of the worst such disasters this century over 250,000 people were drowned in Bangladesh in 1970. The people of that country experienced another storm of similar proportions in 1991 and smaller surges are a regular occurrence there.

The increase in storm intensity during recent years has been tracked by the insurance industry, which has been hit hard by recent disasters. Until the mid-1980s, it was widely thought that windstorms with insured losses exceeding one thousand million U.S. dollars were only possible, if at all, in the United States. But the gales that hit western Europe in October 1987 heralded a series of windstorm disasters which make losses of 10 thousand million dollars seem commonplace. Hurricane Andrew, for instance, left in its wake insured losses estimated at 16 thousand million dollars . . . The rate of economic loss has risen by a factor of four since the 1960s while the increase in insured losses is almost tenfold. Although some of this increase is due to the growth in population over this period in particularly vulnerable areas, a significant part of it seems to have arisen from the increased storminess in the late 1980s and early 1990s.

Windstorms are by no means the only weather and climate extremes that cause disasters. Floods due to unusually intense or prolonged rainfall or droughts because of long periods of reduced rainfall (or its complete absence) can be even more devastating to human life and property. These events occur frequently in many parts of the world especially during in the tropics and subtropics. There have been notable examples during the last decade. In 1988, the highest flood levels ever recorded occurred in Bangladesh; 80 per cent of the entire country was affected. The Yangtze River region of China experienced a devastating flood in 1991. In 1993, flood waters rose to levels higher than ever recorded in the region of Mississippi and Missouri rivers in the United States, flooding an equivalent in size to one of the Great Lakes. Large areas of Africa, both north and south, and of Australia have had droughts on a scale and for longer periods than any in living memory.

Because of the likely locations of floods and droughts, they often bear most heavily on the most vulnerable in the world, who can have little resilience to major disasters . . .

The El Niño Event

Rainfall patterns which lead to floods and droughts in tropical and semi-tropical areas are strongly influenced by the surface temperature of the oceans around the world, particularly the pattern of ocean surface temperature in the Pacific off the coast of South America. About every three to five years a large area of warmer water appears and persists for a year or more. Because they usually occur around Christmas these are known as El Niño ("the boy child") events. They have been well known for centuries to the countries along the coast of South America because of their devastating effect on the fishing industry; the warm top waters of the ocean prevent the nutrients from lower, colder levels required by fish from reaching the surface.

A particularly intense El Niño occurred in 1982–83; the anomalous highs in ocean surface temperature compared to the average reached 7°C. Droughts and floods somewhere in almost all the continents were associated with that El Niño. Like many events associated with weather and climate, El Niños often differ very much in their detailed character. For instance, the El Niño event which began in 1990 and reached maturity early in 1992, apart from some weakening in mid-1992, continued to be dominated by the warm phase until 1995. The exceptional floods in the central United States and in the Andes, and the droughts in Australia and Africa, are probably linked with this unusually protracted El Niño . . .

The Effect of Volcanic Eruptions on Temperature Extremes

Volcanoes inject enormous quantities of dust and gases into the upper atmosphere. Large amounts of sulphur dioxide are included, which through photochemical reactions using the sun's energy are transformed to sulphuric acid and sulphate particles. Typically these particles remain in the stratosphere (the region of atmosphere above about 10 km in altitude) for several years before they fall into the lower atmosphere and are quickly washed out by rainfall. During this period they disperse around the whole globe and cut out some of the radiation from the sun, thus tending to cool the lower atmosphere.

One of the largest volcanic eruptions this century was that from Mount Pinatubo in the Philippines on 12 June 1991 which injected about 20 million tonnes of sulphur dioxide into the stratosphere together with the enormous amounts of dust. This stratospheric dust caused spectacular sunsets around the world for many months following the eruption. The amount of radiation from the sun reaching the lower atmosphere fell by about 2 percent. Global average temperatures lower by about a quarter of a degree Celsius were experienced for the following two years. There is also evidence that some of the unusual weather patterns of 1991 and 1992, for instance unusually cold winters in the Middle East and mild winters in western Europe, were linked with effects of the volcanic dust.

Vulnerable to Change

Over the centuries different human communities have adapted to their particular climate; any large change to the average climate tends to bring stress of one kind or another. It is particularly the extreme climate events and climate disasters which emphasize the importance of climate to our lives and which demonstrate to countries around the world their vulnerability to climate change—a vulnerability which is enhanced by rapidly increasing demands on resources.

But the question must be asked: how remarkable are these events? Do they point to a changing climate due to human activities? Do they provide evidence for global warming because of the increased carbon dioxide and other greenhouse gases being emitted into the atmosphere by burning fossil fuels?

Here a note of caution must be sounded. The range of normal natural climate variation is large. Climate extremes are nothing new. Climate records are continually being broken. In fact, a month without a broken record somewhere would itself be something of a record! Changes in climate, which indicate a genuine long-term trend, can only be identified after many years.

However, we know for sure that, because of human activities, especially the burning of fossil fuels, carbon dioxide in the atmosphere has been increasing over the past two hundred years and more substantially over the past fifty years. To identify climate change related to this carbon dioxide increase, we need to look for trends in global warming over similar lengths of time. They are long compared with both the memories of a generation and the period for which accurate and detailed records exist. Although, therefore, it can be ascertained that there has been more storminess, for instance, in the region of the north Atlantic during the late 1980s and early 1990s than there was in the previous two decades, it is not clear whether those years were that exceptional compared with other periods in the previous hundred years. There is even more difficulty in tracking detailed climate trends in many other parts of the world, owing to the lack of adequate records; further, trends in the frequency of rare events are very difficult to detect.

The generally cold period worldwide during the 1960s and early 1970s caused speculation that the world was heading for an ice age. A British television programme about climate change called "The Ice Age Cometh" was prepared in the early 1970s and widely screened—but the cold trend soon came to an end. We must not be misled by our relatively short memories . . .

During the last few years, as the occurrence of extreme events has made the public much more aware of environmental issues, scientists in their turn have become somewhat more sure about just what human activities are doing to the climate . . .

The Problem of Global Warming

Human industry and other activities such as deforestation are emitting increasing quantities of gases, in particular the gas carbon dioxide, into the atmosphere. Every year these emissions currently add to the carbon already present in atmospheric carbon dioxide a further seven thousand million tonnes, much of which is likely to remain there for a period of a hundred years or more. Because carbon dioxide is a good absorber of heat radiation coming from the Earth's surface, increased carbon dioxide acts like a blanket over the surface, keeping it warmer than it would otherwise be. With the increased temperature the amount of water vapour in the atmosphere also increases, providing more of a blanket effect and causing it to be even warmer.

Being kept warmer may sound appealing to those of us who live in cool climates. However, an increase in global temperature will lead to global climate change. If the change were small and occurred slowly enough we would almost certainly be able to adapt to it. However, with the rapid expansion taking place in the world's industry the change is unlikely to either be small or slow. The estimate I present . . . in the absence of efforts to curb the rise in the emissions of carbon dioxide, the global average temperature will rise by about a quarter of a degree Celsius every ten years—or about two and a half degrees in a century.

This may not sound very much, especially when it is compared with normal temperature variations from day to night or between one day and the next. But it is not the temperature at one place but the temperature averaged over the whole globe. The predicted rate of change of two and a half degrees a century is probably faster than the global average temperature has changed at any time over the past ten thousand years. And as there is a difference in global average temperature of only about five or six degrees between the coldest part of an ice age and the warm period in between ice ages, we can see that a few degrees in this global average can represent a big change in climate.

Not all the climate change will in the end be adverse. While some parts of the world experience more frequent or more severe droughts or floods, other parts perhaps in the sub-arctic, may become more habitable. Even there, though, the likely rate of change will cause problems: large damage to buildings will occur in regions of melting permafrost, and trees in sub-arctic forests, like trees elsewhere, will need time to adapt to new climactic regimes.

Scientists are confident about the fact of global warming and climate change due to human activities. However, substantial uncertainty remains about just how large the warming will be and what will be the patterns of change in different parts of the world. Although some indications can be given, scientists cannot yet say with a lot of detail which regions will be the most affected and in what way. Intensive research is needed to improve the confidence in scientific predictions.

Uncertainty and Response

Until the predictions improve to the point where they can be used as a clear guide to action, politicians and others making decisions are faced with the need to weigh scientific uncertainty against the cost of the various actions which could be taken in response to the threat of climate change. Some action can be taken easily at relatively little cost (or even at a net saving of cost), for instance, the development of programmes to conserve and save energy, and many schemes for reducing deforestation and encouraging the planting of trees. Other actions, such as a large shift to energy sources which do not lead to significant carbon dioxide emissions (for example, renewable sources—biomass, hydro, wind or solar energy) in both the developed and the developing countries of the world will take some time. But here, too, a start can be made. What is important is that plans are made now in preparation for the major changes that will almost certainly be required.

Source Notes

Note to Reader: The following source notes correlated directly to five tables and graphs that were excluded from the extract; however, because they offer valuable information about how the author arrived at his general thesis, they have been included for your reference.

1.   From *World Climate News*, No. 1, June 1992: World Meteorological Organization, Geneva.
2.   After B.V. Shah, 1983, quoted in "Natural Disaster Reduction: How Meteorological Services Can Help," *WMO*, No. 722, 1989, World Meteorological Organization, Geneva.
3.   From G. Berz and K. Conrad, "Winds of Change," *The Review*, June 1993, pp. 32–35.
4.   From "The Role of the World Meteorological Organization in the International Decade for Natural Disaster Reduction" *WMO*, No. 745, 1990, World Meteorological Organization, Geneva.

5.   Adapted from T. Y. Canby, "El Niño's Ill Wind," *National Geographic Magazine*, 1984, pp. 144–183.

In this groundbreaking new hypothesis, science writer and former University of Virginia professor William E. Ruddiman suggests that human influence on Earth's climate began thousands of years before most people imagine—some 8,000 years ago, in fact. In this article, Ruddiman posits that the advent of agriculture, specifically the cultivation of rice in southern Asia and the deforestation of Europe, produced a greater rise in methane and carbon dioxide (CO_2) gases than is currently attributed to the advancements of the Industrial Revolution. While his theory remains controversial, especially since it concludes that the same early rise in atmospheric gases actually made human survival possible, the scientific community continues to consider this and similar theories. Ruddiman recently published a book about early human involvement in climate change called Plows, Plagues, and Petroleum: How Humans Took Control of Climate. *—RC*

"How Did Humans First Alter Global Climate?"
by William E. Ruddiman
Scientific American, March 2005

The scientific consensus that human actions first began to have a warming effect on the earth's climate within the past century has become part of the public perception as well. With the advent of coalburning factories and power plants, industrial societies began releasing carbon dioxide (CO_2) and other greenhouse gases into the air. Later, motor vehicles added to such emissions. In this scenario, those of us who have lived during the industrial era are responsible not only for the gas buildup in the atmosphere but also for at least part of the accompanying global warming trend. Now, though, it seems our ancient agrarian ancestors may have begun adding these gases to the atmosphere many millennia ago, thereby altering the earth's climate long before anyone thought.

New evidence suggests that concentrations of CO_2 started rising about 8,000 years ago, even though natural trends indicate they should have been dropping. Some 3,000 years later the same thing happened to methane, another heat-trapping gas. The consequences of these surprising rises have been profound. Without them, current temperatures in northern parts of North America and Europe would be cooler by three to four degrees Celsius—enough to make agriculture difficult. In addition, an incipient ice age—marked by the appearance of small ice caps—would probably have begun several thousand years ago in parts of northeastern Canada. Instead, the earth's climate has remained relatively warm and stable in recent millennia.

Until a few years ago, these anomalous reversals in greenhouse gas trends and their resulting effects on climate had escaped notice. But after studying the problem for some time, I realized that about 8,000 years ago the gas trends stopped following the pattern that would be predicted from their past long-term behavior, which had been marked by regular cycles. I concluded that human activities tied to farming—primarily agricultural deforestation and crop irrigation—must have added the extra CO_2 and the methane to the atmosphere. These activities explained both the reversals in gas trends and the ongoing increases right up to the start of the industrial era. Since then, modern technological innovations have brought about even faster rises in greenhouse gas concentrations.

My claim that human contributions have been altering the earth's climate for millennia is provocative and controversial. Other scientists have reacted to this proposal with the mixture of enthusiasm and skepticism that is typical when novel ideas are put forward, and testing of this hypothesis is now under way.

The Current View

This new idea builds on decades of advances in understanding long-term climate change. Scientists have known since the 1970s that three predictable variations in the earth's orbit around the sun have exerted the dominant control over long-term global climate for millions of years. As a consequence of these orbital cycles (which operate over 100,000, 41,000 and 22,000 years), the amount of solar radiation reaching various parts of the globe during a given season can differ by more than 10 percent. Over the past three million years, these regular changes in the amount of sunlight reaching the planet's surface have produced a long sequence of ice ages (when great areas of Northern Hemisphere continents were covered with ice) separated by short, warm interglacial periods.

Dozens of these climactic sequences occurred over the million of years when hominids were slowly evolving toward anatomically modern humans. At the end of the most recent glacial period, the ice sheets that had blanketed northern Europe and North America for the previous 100,000 years shrank and, by 6,000 years ago, had disappeared. Soon after, our ancestors built cities, invented writing and founded religions. Many scientists credit much of the progress of civilization to this naturally warm gap between less favorable glacial intervals, but in my opinion this view is far from the full story.

In recent years, cores of ice drilled in the Antarctic and Greenland ice sheets have provided extremely valuable evidence about the earth's past climate, including changes in the concentrations of the greenhouse gases. A three-kilometer-long ice core retrieved from Vostok Station in Antarctica during the 1990s contained trapped bubbles of ancient air that revealed concentrations of CO_2 and methane rose and fell in regular pattern virtually all of the past 400,000 years.

Particularly noteworthy was that these increases and decreases in greenhouse gases occurred at the same intervals as variations in the intensity of solar radiation and the size of the ice sheets. For example, methane concentrations fluctuate mainly at a 22,000-year tempo of an orbital cycle called precession. As the earth spins on its rotation axis, it wobbles like a top, slowly swinging the Northern Hemisphere closer to and then farther away from the sun. When this precessional wobble brings the northern continents nearest the sun during the summertime, the atmosphere gets a notable boost of methane from its primary natural source—the decomposition of plant matter in wetlands.

After wetland vegetation flourishes in late summer, it then dies, decays and emits carbon in the form of methane, sometimes called swamp gas. Periods of maximum summer-time heating enhance methane production in two primary ways: In southern Asia, the warmth draws additional moisture-laden air in from the Indian Ocean, driving strong tropical monsoons that flood regions that might otherwise stay dry. In far northern Asia and Europe, hot summers thaw boreal wetlands for longer periods of the year. Both processes enable more vegetation to grow, decompose and emit methane every 22,000 years. When the Northern Hemisphere veers farther from the sun, methane emissions start to decline. They bottom out 11,000 years later—the point in the cycle when Northern Hemisphere summers receive the least solar radiation.

Unexpected Reversals

Examining records from the Vostok ice core closely, I spotted something odd about the recent part of the record. Early in previous interglacial intervals, the methane concentration typically reached a peak of almost 700 parts per billion (ppb) as precession brought summer radiation to a maximum. The same thing happened 11,000 years ago, just as the current interglacial period began. Also in agreement with prior cycles, the methane concentration then declined by 100 ppb as summer sunshine subsequently waned. Had the recent trend continued to mimic older interglacial intervals, it would have fallen to a value near 450 ppb during the current minimum in summer heating. Instead the trend reversed direction 5,000 years ago and rose gradually back to almost 700 ppb just before the start of the industrial era. In short, the methane concentration rose when it should have fallen, and it ended up 250 ppb higher than the equivalent point in earlier cycles.

Like methane, CO_2 had behaved unexpectedly over the past several thousand years. Although a complex combination of all three orbital cycles controls CO_2 variations, the trends during previous interglacial intervals were all surprisingly similar to one another. Concentrations peaked at 275 to 300 parts per million (ppm) early in each warm period, even more before the last remnants of the great ice sheets finished melting. The CO_2 levels then fell steadily over the next 15,000 years to an average of about 224 ppm. During the current interglacial interval, CO_2 concentrations reached the expected peak around 10,500 years ago, and, just as anticipated, began a similar decline. But instead of continuing to drop steadily through modern times, the trend reversed direction 8,000 years ago. By the start of the industrial era, the concentration had risen to 285 ppm—roughly 40 ppm higher than expected from the earlier behavior.

What could explain these unexpected reversals in the natural trends of both methane and CO_2? Other investigators suggested that natural factors in the climate system provided the answer. The methane increase has been ascribed to expansion of wetlands in Arctic regions and the CO_2 rise to natural losses of carbon-rich vegetation on the continents, as well as to changes in the chemistry of the ocean. Yet it struck me that these explanations were doomed to fail for a simple reason. During the four preceding interglaciations, the major factors thought to influence greenhouse gas concentrations in the atmosphere were nearly the same as in recent millennia. The northern ice sheets had melted, northern forests had reoccupied the land uncovered by ice, meltwater from the ice had returned sea level to its high interglacial position, and solar radiation driven the earth's orbit had increased and then began to decrease in the same way.

Why, then, would the gas concentrations have fallen during the last four interglaciations yet risen only during the current one? I concluded that something new to the natural workings of the climate system must have been operating during the past several thousand years.

The Human Connection

The most plausible "new factor" operating in the climate system during the present interglaciation is farming. The basic timeline of agricultural innovations is well known. Agriculture originated in the Fertile Crescent region of the eastern Mediterranean around 11,000 years ago, shortly thereafter in northern China, and several thousand years later in the Americas. Through subsequent millennia it spread to other regions and increased in sophistication. By 2,000 years ago, every crop food eaten today was being cultivated somewhere in the world.

Several farming activities generate methane. Rice paddies flooded by irrigation generate methane for the same reason that natural wetlands do—vegetation decomposes in the stagnate standing water. Methane is also released as farmers burn grasslands to attract game and promote growth of berries. In addition, people and their domesticated animals emit methane with feces and belches. All these factors probably contributed to a gradual rise in methane as human populations grew slowly, but only one process seems likely to have accounted for the abruptness of the reversal from a natural methane decline to an unexpected rise around 5,000 years ago—the onset of rice irrigation in southern Asia.

Farmers began flooding lowlands near rivers to grow wet-adapted strains of rice around 5,000 years ago in the south of China. With extensive floodplains lying within easy reach of several large rivers, it makes sense that broad swaths of land could have been flooded soon after the technique was discovered, thus explaining the quick shift in the methane trend. Historical records also indicate a steady expansion in rice irrigation throughout the interval when methane values were rising. By 3,000 years ago the technique had spread south into Indochina and west to the Ganges River Valley in India, further increasing methane emissions. After 2,000 years, farmers began to construct rice paddies on the steep hillsides of Southeast Asia.

Future research may provide quantitative estimates of the amount of land irrigated and methane generated through this 5,000-year interval. Such estimates will probably be difficult to come by, however, because repeated irrigation of the same areas into modern times has probably disturbed much of the earlier evidence. For now, my case rests mainly on the basic fact that the methane trend went the "wrong way" and that farmers began to irrigate wetlands at just the right time to explain this wrong-way trend.

Another common practice tied to farming—deforestation—provides a plausible explanation for the start of the anomalous CO_2 trend. Growing crops in naturally forested areas requires cutting trees, and farmers began to clear forests for this purpose in Europe and China by 8,000 years ago, initially with axes made of stone and later from bronze and then iron. Whether the fallen trees were burned or left to rot, their carbon would have soon oxidized and ended up in the atmosphere as CO_2.

Scientists have precisely dated evidence that Europeans began growing nonindigenous crop plants such as wheat, barley and peas in naturally forested areas just as the CO_2 trend reversed 8,000 years ago. Remains of these plants, initially cultivated in the Near East, first appear in lake sediments in southeastern Europe and then spread west and north over the next several thousand years. During this interval, silt and clay began to wash into rivers and lakes from denuded hillsides at increasing rates, further attesting to ongoing forest clearance.

The most unequivocal evidence of early and extensive deforestation lies in a unique historical document—the *Domesday Book*. This survey of England, ordered by William the Conqueror, reported that 90 percent of the natural forest in lowland, agricultural regions was cleared as of AD 1086. The survey also counted 1.5 million people living in England at the time, indicating that an average density of 10 people per square kilometer was sufficient to eliminate the forests. Because the advanced civilizations of the major river valleys of China and India had reached much higher population densities several thousand years prior, many historical ecologists have concluded that these regions were heavily deforested some two or even three thousand years ago. In summary, Europe and southern Asia had been heavily deforested long before the start of the industrial era, and the clearance process was well under way throughout the time of the unusual CO_2 rise.

An Ice Age Prevented?

If farmers were responsible for greenhouse gas anomalies this large—250 ppb for methane and 40 ppm for CO_2 by the 1700s—the effect of their practices on the earth's climate would have been substantial. Based on the average sensitivity shown by a range of climate models, the combined effect from these anomalies would have been an average warming of almost 0.8 degree C just before the industrial era. That amount is larger than the 0.6 degree C warming measured during the past century—implying that the effect of early farming on climate rivals or even exceeds the combined changes registered during the time of rapid industrialization.

How did this dramatic warming effect escape recognition for so long? The main reason is that it was masked by natural climactic changes in the opposite direction. The earth's orbital cycles were driving a simultaneous natural cooling trend, especially at high northern latitudes. The net temperature change was a gradual summer cooling trend lasting until the 1800s.

Had greenhouse gases been allowed to follow their natural tendency to decline, the resulting cooling would have augmented the one being driven by the drop in summer radiation, and this planet would have become considerably cooler than it is now. To explore this possibility, I joined with Stephen J. Vavrus and John E. Kutzbach of the University of Wisconsin–Madison to use a climate model to predict modern-day temperature in the absence of all human-generated greenhouse gases. The model simulates the average state of the earth's climate—including temperature and precipitation—in response to different initial conditions.

For our experiment, we reduced the greenhouse gas levels in the atmosphere to the values they would have reached today without early farming or industrial emissions. The resulting simulation showed that our planet would be almost two degrees C cooler than it is now—a significant difference. In comparison, the global mean temperature at the last glacial maximum 20,000 years ago was only five to six degrees C colder than it is today. In effect, current temperatures would be well on the way toward typical glacial temperatures had it not been for the greenhouse gas contributions from early farming practices and later industrialization.

I had also initially proposed that new ice sheets might have begun to form in the far north if this natural cooling had been allowed to proceed. Other researchers had shown previously that parts of far northeastern Canada might be ice covered today if the world were cooler by just 1.5 to two degrees C—the same amount of cooling that our experiment suggested has been offset by the greenhouse gas anomalies. The later modeling effort with my Wisconsin colleagues showed that snow would now persist into late summer in two areas of northeastern Canada: Baffin Island, just east of the mainland, and Labrador, farther south. Because any snow that survives throughout the summer will accumulate in thicker piles year by year and eventually become glacial ice, these results suggest that a new ice age would have begun in northeast Canada several millennia ago, at least on a small scale.

This conclusion is startlingly different from the traditional view that human civilization blossomed within a period of warmth that nature provided. As I see it, nature would have cooled the earth's climate, but our ancestors kept it warm by discovering agriculture.

Implications for the Future

The conclusion that humans prevented a cooling and arguably stopped the initial stage of a glacial cycle bears directly on a long-running dispute over what global climate has in store for us in the near future. Part of the reason that policymakers had trouble embracing the initial predictions of global warming in the 1980s was that a number of scientists had spent the previous decade telling everyone almost exactly the opposite—that an ice age was on its way. Based on the new confirmation that orbital variations control the growth and decay of ice sheets, some scientists studying these longer-scale changes had reasonably concluded that the next ice age might be only a few hundred or at most a few thousand years away.

In subsequent years, however, investigators found that greenhouse gas concentrations were rising rapidly and that the earth's climate was warming, at least in part because of the gas increases. This evidence convinced most scientists that the relatively near-future (the next century or two) would be dominated by global warming rather than by global cooling. This revised prediction, based on an improved understanding of the climate system, led some policymakers to discount all forecasts—whether of global warming or an impending ice age—as untrustworthy.

My findings add a new wrinkle to each scenario. If anything, such forecasts of an "impending" ice age were actually understated; new ice sheets should have begun to grow several millennia ago. The ice failed to grow because human-induced global warming actually began far earlier than previously thought—well before the industrial era.

In these kinds of hotly contested topics that touch on public policy, scientific results are often used for opposing ends. Global-warming skeptics could cite my work as evidence that human-generated greenhouse gases played a beneficial role for several thousand years by keeping the earth's climate more hospitable that it would otherwise have been. Others might counter that if so few humans with relatively primitive technologies were able to alter the course of climate so significantly, then we have reason to be concerned about the current rise of greenhouse gases to unparalleled concentrations at unprecedented rates.

The rapid warming of the past century is probably destined to persist for at least 200 years, until the economically accessible fossil fuels become scarce. Once that happens, the earth's climate should begin to cool gradually as the deep ocean slowly absorbs the pulse of excess CO_2 from human activities. Whether global climate will cool enough to produce the long-overdue glaciation or remain warm enough to avoid that fate is impossible to predict.

Orbital Controls over Greenhouse Gases

Natural variations in the earth's orbit, such as those related to precession, redistribute the sunlight that reaches the globe over long timescales. For the past million years, these subtle changes have driven major dips and swells in atmospheric concentrations of methane and carbon dioxide. Although scientists do not fully understand why, global concentrations of these greenhouse gases respond mainly to changes that occur during summer in the Northern Hemisphere, the time of year when the North Pole is pointed most directly at the sun.

CHAPTER TWO

PEOPLE, PLACES, AND ENVIRONMENTS: SPECIFIC EFFECTS OF GLOBAL WARMING

The effects of global warming include more than rising temperatures; in fact, all changes in climate are interrelated and can cause a variety of events that could possibly alter our entire way of life. In this article by Curtis Abraham, British geologist John Reynolds urges the need for updated research into the rate at which glaciers are melting and the danger this poses to nearby communities. As the glaciers melt, he explains, small lakes are created that often swell and flood lower-level areas. In some cases, such as in the Himalayas, this could mean massive flooding and landslides that could potentially kill millions of people. A recent report by the United Nations Environment Programme named more than forty glacial lakes in the Himalayan kingdoms of Bhutan and Nepal "that are filling so rapidly they could burst their banks in as little as five years' time." Since the economies of both kingdoms are based almost solely on agriculture and forestry, flooding of this magnitude would be disastrous. In addition to the threat of catastrophic flooding, the disappearance of glaciers often means that regions once powered by hydroelectricity will no longer have use of the same resources. —RC

"Glacial Meltdown Threatens People Downstream"
by Curtis Abraham
New Scientist, November 2, 2002

It was a close encounter with death that changed John Reynolds's life. He describes how, as a young geography student on a field trip in northern Norway, he watched helplessly as a glacial lake burst its banks and a wall of water rushed down the valley towards him. "I was stranded on one side as the flood made a 10-metre-wide gap in the road. The rest of the team was on the other side. Suddenly one of them shouted to me to get back. I was within seconds of being washed away as the road disappeared beneath my feet. I ended up just a metre away from the edge. It would have been the end for me."

Instead, it was the beginning of a lifelong obsession that has made Reynolds probably the world's greatest expert on these glacial time bombs and how to evaluate and defuse them. Today he knows that the power of a bursting lake can be awesome, throwing huge boulders long distances. "Much of the water moves down the valley in a single gigantic wave carrying everything in its path," he says. In a constricted valley, the wave doesn't dissipate, but keeps on going, sometimes for hundreds of kilometres. In 1964, for example, when a glacial lake in Tibet burst and destroyed a highway, trucks from the road turned up 70 kilometres away. During the 20th century, around 32,000 people were killed and millions of dollars worth of infrastructure such as roads and hydroelectric plants were destroyed by glacial disasters, many of them involving bursting lakes.

Reynolds's dire warning is that things are set to get much worse. As global warming gathers pace, thousands of glaciers that grew during the "little ice age" from 1500 to 1800 are melting fast and creating their own lakes. Recent estimates suggest there are 1,500 glacial lakes in Peru, 2,000 in Nepal and nearly 3,000 in the tiny Himalayan kingdom of Bhutan. There may be 800 more in the Italian Alps alone. Nobody has got round to even estimating the number in Pakistan, India, Tibet, Kazakhstan or Bolivia. Most are not an immediate hazard. But earlier this year a report from the UN Environment Programme (UNEP) named 44 glacial lakes in Bhutan and Nepal "that are filling so rapidly they could burst their banks in as little as five years' time." The report's author, Surendra Shrestha, warned: "These are the ones we know about. Who knows how many others elsewhere in the Himalayas and across the world are in a similar critical state?"

Although the water from melting glaciers often simply runs down to the sea, in many cases the valley below is dammed by a pile of debris, or moraine, deposited at the glacier's end before it began retreating. These unstable moraines can be more than 100 metres high and hold back a meltwater lake several kilometres long. Potentially catastrophic lakes can form from nothing in less than five years. "Often the first time the existence of a lake becomes apparent is when it floods communities downstream," says Reynolds. "In the 1950s we had about one burst a decade. In the 1990s, it was three a decade. By 2010 I think we will be talking about one every year."

Reynolds predicts that the 21st century could see hundreds of millions dead and tens of billions of dollars in damage. The problem is made worse because more and more people are living in the narrow valleys beneath the lakes. And they are being joined by increasing numbers of tourists, usually oblivious to the threat as they marvel at mighty glaciers reflected in the crystal waters.

Methods of assessing the risk of these lakes bursting are often crude, says Reynolds. "Many supposed experts, including some working for UNEP, seem to just go looking on satellite images for water, and when they find it, pronounce it unsafe. Then they depart, leaving local people in sometimes quite unnecessary fear."

The most dangerous lakes, says Reynolds, are ones that have a high but narrow moraine with water almost to the brim, perching precariously above a steep valley. The moraine may be leaking or contain a block of ice that could melt, making a hole in the dam below the water line. Most dangerous of all, there may be an unstable bank or a cliff of melting ice that could fall into the lake, causing a tidal wave that would breach the moraine.

Reynolds, who runs a geological consulting company in north Wales, has been heavily involved in efforts to identify and stabilise dangerous lakes in both Peru and, more recently, the Himalayas. He claims part of the credit for saving the lives of some 25,000 people in 1989. He negotiated emergency British aid to airlift in siphons to lower a Peruvian glacial lake beneath the Hualcan glacier as a block of ice in the moraine melted, threatening the town of Carhuaz, nestled in a valley 2,000 metres below. "We probably had less than two months before disaster struck," he says.

That particular operation was a success, but sometimes trying to solve the problem can make it worse. "One of the biggest hazards," says Reynolds, "is botched attempts to empty dangerous lakes, especially by digging a channel or tunnel through the moraine." In 1993, Reynolds returned to the Hualcan glacier to watch Peruvian engineers dig a tunnel to lower the lake by a further 20 metres. He realised that the water pressure in the tunnel during the discharge would be so great that the moraine would burst. His solution was to dig a series of tunnels to lower the lake in five-metre stages, reducing the pressure on the moraine. The inhabitants of Carhuaz were saved for a second time.

Other efforts have been less fortunate. In 1950, Peruvian engineers were draining Lake Jancarurish at the toe of the Kogan glacier. As the water level dropped, a tongue of ice that had been floating on the water surface was left in mid-air and broke off the glacier. The crash sent a giant wave across the lake, bursting through the moraine. Some 10 million cubic metres of water flooded into the valley below. Around 500 people, mostly project workers, were drowned.

Reynolds fears that a combination of poor survey work and short-sighted engineering could lead to an even worse disaster in Bhutan. The Lunana valley—on the route of the popular "snowman trek"—contains probably the most perilous complex of glacial lakes in the Himalayas. It includes Thorthormi and Raphstreng, two particularly fast-growing lakes. Thorthormi is 65 metres vertically above Raphstreng and held back by a moraine less than 30 metres wide. If the moraine breaks, Thorthormi will pour into Raphstreng, sending the water from both lakes crashing down the valley. "Around 48,000 people live in the valley downstream. Whole communities would be drowned," says Reynolds.

Photographs reveal the moraine may already be shifting. And Reynolds claims to have uncovered evidence, missed by

Austrian scientists who surveyed the moraine three years ago, that water is already seeping from Thorthormi into Raphstreng. Recent engineering may be to blame. Two years ago, Indian engineers dug a drainage channel to lower the water in Raphstreng. "My big fear is that by lowering the water level they may have destabilised the moraine," says Reynolds. "I wouldn't be surprised to see a Reuters report of a disaster there within a year."

If it does happen, a catastrophic outburst at Bhutan's Lunana lakes will send lethal floods across the border into India. This raises the issue of who should pay for any engineering solution to such problems. Bhutan and India enjoy reasonably good relations, but in other regions of the Himalayas where a glacial outburst in one country threatens people in another, the situation is potentially explosive in political terms. An incident in Indian-held Kashmir, for instance, might kill thousands in Pakistan. Scandalously, glaciologists can only guess at the risks for the moment because India recently refused a UNEP research team permission to survey its Kashmiri lakes, on account of security fears.

Around the world, governments are slowly waking up to the danger lurking in the mountains, but even where there is a will to act, the backlog of basic survey work is huge. Nowhere is this more apparent than in Peru, where many large towns lie directly in the path of potential devastation. Peru's state-run hydroelectric company, Electroperu, has drained some 40 lakes in the past half-century and there have been no deaths from lake bursts since 1972. However, it disbanded its mountain safety unit six years ago, following privatisation. Although the unit resumed work less than a year ago under government control, the glaciologist who ran the old survey team, Cesar

Portocarrero, warns: "We no longer have the glacial lakes mapped. New lakes are forming all the time, so the risk of another big disaster grows."

And glacial meltdown brings other problems besides catastrophic floods. Along the length of the Andes, from Colombia to southern Chile, the disappearance of glaciers will soon mean dwindling supplies of hydroelectric power and water, according to Lonnie Thompson of Ohio State University. Cities under threat include the Ecuadorian capital, Quito, which is watered by a glacier on Antisana mountain that has shrunk by a third in 40 years, and the Peruvian capital Lima, which depends on glacial meltwater to maintain the River Rimac's year-round flow across the coastal desert. "In Bolivia, water supplies for half the country's population are threatened if the glaciers disappear," says Bernard Francou of the Paris-based Institute for Development Research, who predicted in a study published last year that 80 per cent of the country's glaciers would be gone by 2020.

It's a similar story in the Himalayas. The Gangorti glacier at the head of the River Ganges, for instance, is retreating at a rate of 30 metres per year. Today, the extra meltwater each spring brings floods downstream. But as the glaciers begin to disappear in the coming decades, the river flows will become less reliable and eventually diminish, bringing widespread water shortages, according to Syed Hasnain of Jawaharlal Nehru University in Delhi, who has studied the glaciers for the International Commission on Snow and Ice. Dry-season flows of water sustained by Himalayan glaciers could be gone in 30 years.

Many of Europe's great rivers such as the Rhine, Rhône, Po and Danube also rely partly on glacial meltwater to sustain their summer flows. Researchers may eventually conclude that the floods in central Europe earlier this year had as much to do with fast-melting glaciers as heavy rains. But, says David Collins from Salford University, "when all the ice goes, the summer flow of the rivers will be almost entirely dependent on rainfall. And under global warming, rainfall in southern Europe is set to reduce."

In the Alps, tourism is already suffering as a result of glacial meltdown. Austrian ski resorts, including Kitzbühel and Zell-am-See, are close to being abandoned because of insufficient snow. In Switzerland, St Moritz and Klosters could soon lose their lower pistes. Some resorts have already shut down, and at many others the skiing season is weeks shorter than it was just a decade ago.

Of course, the root of all these problems is global warming, and the decline of Europe's ski industry seems inevitable unless we can reverse the warming trend. But Reynolds points out that we already have the know-how to alleviate some of the worst effects of glacial meltdown. Proper engineering of potentially dangerous lakes can both save lives downstream and turn the lakes into dependable sources of energy and water. Electroperu has in the past few decades converted several dangerous lakes into safe economic assets by replacing their unstable moraines with concrete dams. In essence, the world's frozen water towers could be gradually replaced by reservoirs in this way. And Reynolds sees this incentive as the way to inject investment into saving lives in the mountains.

The idea of holding even more water in the mountains might sound foolhardy, but with good glaciology to ensure no unpleasant surprises, it's perfectly possible. "We have the expertise to prevent deaths from glacial lakes," says Reynolds. "The trouble is we so rarely get the chance. I keep scanning the headlines fearing the next disaster."

New information has emerged from an experiment by more than 800 scientists. Tropical ecosystems such as the Amazon rain forest, 2.3 million square miles (6 million square kilometers) of South American wetlands, could literally dry up because of rising temperatures and deforestation. According to the study, a lesser-known contributor to this changing environment is the physical alteration of the region's rain clouds, a factor that was unknown to scientists when the Large Scale Biosphere/Atmosphere Experiment began in 1999. In one of the climate models used for the ongoing experiment, up to 60 percent of the rain forest could turn into savanna by 2100, according to Claudio Angelo, science writer and editor of the Folha de S. Paulo, *a daily newspaper in Brazil.* —RC

"Punctuated Disequilibrium"
by Claudio Angelo
Scientific American, February, 2005

With a bit more warmth and extra fertilizer, a plant can go from limp to lush. But all the good things for flora are meaningless without water. According to recent analyses, large parts of the Amazon rain forests, which sprawls across an area about as large as western Europe, could end up turning into dry savannas—a state from which there may be no turning back even if the climate returned to normal.

This somber prediction comes out of the latest findings of the Large Scale Biosphere/Atmosphere Experiment in Amazonia, the most ambitious field project ever done in a tropical ecosystem. Since 1999 the experiment, sponsored by the Brazilian government, NASA and the European Union, has brought together 800 scientists, who have been probing the six-million-square-kilometer jungle with instrument-laden towers, airplanes and satellites in a quest to understand how the forest works.

The researchers still have a long way to go for a complete picture. But they think they now know enough to begin to assess how the complex Amazon ecosystem will react to global warming, increased carbon dioxide (which acts as fertilizer) and other changes. Two studies in the project suggest a trend toward the formation of savannas at the eastern and southern parts of the forest.

A key factor is deforestation, which alone in the eastern Amazon could tip the ecosystem toward a drier state. Plants in that region, which is naturally drier than other parts of the forest, help to keep moisture in the area by recycling water through evaporation and transpiration. Without the flora, drought sets in. The mean temperature also goes up.

Change in land may also dry up the forest in a less straightforward way: by altering the physical properties of rain clouds. In a series of experiments carried out with aircraft flying through smoke plumes during forest fires, a team lead by physicist Maria Assunção da Silva Dias of the National Institute for Space Research and her colleague Paulo Artaxo of the University of São Paulo has found that smoke aerosols probably inhibit formation of big water drops, producing clouds that are incapable of rain.

Climatologist Carlos A. Nobre, a leading scientist at the Brazilian National Institute for Space Research, has factored the effects of deforestation and global warming into a computer model that couples vegetation changes with standard global circulation models. In one of Nobre's scenarios, by 2100, up to 60 percent of the forest will turn into *cerrado*, the type of savanna that dominates the landscape in central Brazil. Such a shift in land cover might be hard to reverse. "We are forcing the forest system into a new state of equilibrium," he says.

The effects of warming by itself are harder to elucidate. But atmospheric scientist Steven C. Wofsy of Harvard University and his colleagues have devised a novel way to estimate the impact of climate change on the current state of the forest. The researchers looked at the likelihood of extreme events, such as abnormal droughts, and matched them to field observations of the drought-sensitive vegetation of Tapajós National Forest in central-eastern Amazonia in the Brazilian state of Pará. They then used their model to generate a simulation spanning 2,500 years and found that forest gives way to *cerrado* when more than 33 years of drought occur in a century. "You end up bisecting the Amazon with savannas," remarks Lucy Hutyra, a member of Wofsy's team.

The take-home message, she says, is that the extremes are more important than the averages. In a global change scenario, the temperature can rise without signs of ecosystem disturbance in the Amazon. But on the scale of centuries, some areas of the forest, such as the Tapajós region, are highly sensitive to variability. "There is a lot of deadwood and fuel for fire," Wofsy explains. "Suppose you have 10 or 20 years in which nothing happens, then one of those droughts strikes and there is a fire. If the fire isn't too severe, the forest recovers. If it comes again in 25 years or 15 years, everything is destroyed."

From butterflies to daffodils, the world's species are changing to adapt to global warming. Mari N. Jensen, a science writer at the University of Arizona, discusses the results of several scientific studies that show how animals and plants are coping with climate change. For example, Jensen reveals startling evidence from a team of Boston biologists that suggests that sixty-six species of New England's plants are now flowering eight days earlier than they did before 1920. Erik Beever, ecologist with the U.S. Geological Survey, agrees that global warming is affecting our ecosystem. In an ongoing survey of the habits of pikas, small rabbitlike creatures, he noted that 28 percent of the pika population at lower elevations had vanished between 1994 and 1999. This finding, Jensen reports, is no longer unique. In one climate model led by two research teams, one at Stanford University and the other at the University of Texas–Austin, 1,700 species from around the globe were analyzed. The results were that "more than 80 percent of the species tested had exhibited range changes (in habitat), phenological changes, or even some behavioral,

physiological, or genetic changes,"; this has been attributed to global warming. —RC

From "Climate Warming Shakes Up Species"
by Mari N. Jensen
BioScience, August 2004

It wasn't just an isolated incident of one very early bird. Since 1980, robins have been steadily showing up in Gothic earlier and earlier. The birds' accelerating eagerness to get to those high-altitude worms coincides with increasingly warm spring temperatures at the lab, located at 2,945 meters elevation in the Colorado Rockies.

The robins are just one sign that spring is busting out all over. In the Northern Hemisphere, scientists and naturalists are noting advances in the timing of a myriad of seasonal events, including the blooming of daffodils, the leafing out of trees, and egg-laying by frogs and birds. Even people have joined in the fun: In England, lawns need mowing earlier than in past years.

Biologists chalk up these and other alterations in plant and animal behavior to global climate change. In the 20th century, the world's temperature rose 0.6 degrees Celsius (°C). Temperatures in the northernmost and southernmost regions increased more than that. Scientists predict that the planet will continue to warm: In 2001, the United Nations' Intergovernmental Panel on Climate Change (IPCC) reported that from 1990 to 2100, the world's temperature is projected to climb an additional 1.4°C to 5.8°C.

One of the pleasures of the natural world—its variety—
makes it difficult for scientists to tease out which biological
responses are due to a long-term warming trend and which are
just year-to-year variations that should be attributed to the
vagaries of weather. Predicting how biological systems will
react as the climate changes is an even greater challenge. But
the more they search, the more scientists find climate-induced
biological changes. Spurred by those findings, other
researchers are forecasting how the world's biota may respond
to additional climate change and which flora and fauna will be
most affected. Climate change, researchers say, is transforming the natural world . . .

Finding Long-Term Biological Records

Herbarium records are one possible source of [changes related
to increased temperatures], say Boston University conservation biologists Richard Primack and Abraham Miller-Rushing.
At Boston's Arnold Arboretum, each individual plant on the
grounds is numbered. Since 1885, arboretum staff have been
making herbarium sheets—flattened, preserved pieces of individual plants that have the plant's identification number and
the collection date. Such specimens are often collected at the
peak of flowering for that particular plant.

Using herbarium sheets, Primack, Miller-Rushing, and
their colleagues compared 229 living plants' flowering dates for
the period 1885 to 2002. A combination of global warming and
urban development warmed the Boston area 1.5°C during that
time period. The team's analysis included species that live more
than a century, such as magnolia, rhododendron, dogwood,
mountain laurel, and cherry. In all, the analysis encompassed 66

species from 37 genera. From 1980 to 2002, the plants flowered eight days earlier than they did from 1900 to 1920, the team reports in an article scheduled for publication in [the August 2004] issue of the *American Journal of Botany*.

"What this study is showing is that plants are very responsive to global warming," says Primack. "And the global warming we are seeing in the Boston area right now gives us a preview or window into what's going to be happening throughout the rest of the United States over the coming decades or centuries."

Flowers are also blooming earlier in England. From 1954 to 2000, the well-known British nature writer Richard Fitter jotted down the time of first flowering, or phenology, for plant species in the vicinity of his home in Oxford, England. Results from the comparison of the flowering dates from 1990–2000 with those from the previous four decades startled Fitter's son Alastair, an ecologist at York University in England.

"I was surprised how strong the effect was," says Alastair Fitter. "Four and a half days in a decade averaged across nearly 400 plant species is astonishing." Some species have advanced their flowering times by more than a month. Alastair and his father published their findings in *Science* in 2002.

Taking notes on natural occurrences isn't just the purview of scientists or nature writers. In Britain, long the home of amateur naturalists, Tim Sparks compiles data gleaned from thousands of inveterate note takers, people he calls "closet phenologists." Sparks says, "These are people that are unaware that other people are recording similar events. Slightly embarrassed by what they do, they are just doing it as a pastime for pure interest." Often the person records just one type of event, such as the date each year that frog spawn first appears in a backyard pond. From about 20 people, Sparks has logs representing 50 years or more of such note taking, and he has many more records of shorter duration. His closet phenologists range from a woman in Norwich who for 40 years has been recording what flowers in her garden every day to people who just note whenever they mow their lawns.

In 1998, Sparks and his colleagues at the Woodland Trust launched a national effort to encourage people to share such data and to collect even more. Sparks, an environmental scientist at the Centre for Ecology and Hydrology in Huntingdon, United Kingdom, says, "Their records—anything up to 50 years long—are now proving very valuable in looking for any signals that might be present." The effort now has about 14,000 people registered to record the timing of various biological events in Britain. Data keepers can either send in paper records or submit their information on the Web site [http://www.phenology.org.uk]. It's the largest such effort in the world, Sparks says, noting that the team now has about 750,000 data points. He anticipates having one million data points sometime soon.

Although some might quibble that the variety of record keepers and methodologies dilute the reliability of the data, Sparks, a statistician by training, says that isn't so. "We're gathering data from such a large number of people that a few inaccurate observations don't really make a great deal of difference. For example, last year we had over three thousand observations on bumblebee[s]."

The message is clear: The climate is changing, and the biota are responding. Compared with Britain's long-term temperature records, which go back to 1659, the 1990s were hotter and drier. Sparks says, "We're breaking records all the time. Last year we had the sunniest February ever, the hottest day ever, the driest October ever. All these records seem to be being broken down in the last 10 years, which is very, very suspicious and helps to suggest that the climate is already changing."

Winter temperatures have increased more than summer temperatures, thereby starting the growing season earlier. "When pressed, I say that spring has advanced by three weeks in the last 50 years in Britain," Sparks says. Even people's behavior has been affected: Although grass didn't normally grow year-round in Britain, now in some places it does. People report having to mow their lawns on Boxing Day, the day after Christmas.

Primack hopes to find the same kinds of records in the Boston area. He and his colleagues have already launched such an effort around Concord, Massachusetts, home of the famed philosopher and naturalist Henry David Thoreau. For a baseline, the researchers use Thoreau's 1851–1858 notes on the flowering of various species of plants. On and off, naturalists and scientists have focused on Concord, making it one of the best-studied towns of its size in the United States, says Primack. The 150-year record that started with Thoreau, while not continuous, is substantial enough that the researchers expect to see more evidence that plants now bloom earlier than they did in the 1850s. Moreover, the Boston University team has started a new data-collection effort focused on

Concord to document other changes in local natural history that have occurred since Thoreau's time.

Warming Climate Means Move or Die

Another way to use naturalists' or museums' records is to revisit sites where specific species historically occurred. As part of his graduate research at the University of Nevada–Reno, Erik Beever studied pikas, small, tailless rabbit relatives that weigh about 150 grams and look a bit like hamsters. In the Great Basin of the American West, pikas live high in the mountains on the rocky talus slopes. From 1994 to 1999, Beever revisited 24 locations in the Great Basin where pikas have been observed between 1898 and 1947, either by noted mammalogist E. Raymond Hall or by other scientists. Beever also surveyed a 25th location that had pikas in 1990.

Beever found that 7 of the original 25 sites (28 percent) no longer had pikas. The pika populations that vanished were those at lower elevations, which suggests that climactic warming is involved. "One of the simplest predictions of climate change is that animals would move either more northward or upslope," says Beever, who is now an ecologist with the US Geological Survey in Corvallis, Oregon. "In the Great Basin, pikas are located in these mountain ranges separated by more-or-less inhospitable valleys." Coupled with the fact that the most peripatetic of pikas generally move less than a kilometer from their birthplaces, Beever says, "they really aren't that able to move more northward."

Although he doesn't rule out direct alteration of habitat, such as that from roads or livestock grazing, beever says thermal changes in the pikas' habitat play a dominant role in the local extinctions. It's actually habitat loss, but of a subtle kind: Pikas don't live in places that are being converted to condos or shopping malls. He says, "If climate change is driving this, there's been an effective change in habitat—taluses that were habitable no longer are."

A similar thing seems to be occurring with desert bighorn sheep. Like pikas, desert bighorns generally stick to their natal mountain range, in this case, isolated, often small, mountains separated from one another by expanses of bleak, blistering-hot Mojave desert. Conservation biologist Clinton W. Epps, a graduate student at the University of California-Berkley, reviewed the 1994 survey data for 80 sites in the southern California desert where bighorns were found historically. In addition, he visited about half of the sites and scouted for sheep. By the mid-1990s, 30 of the 80 sheep populations were extinct.

"Most of those desert populations are not suffering a lot of direct human impact," Epps says. "Either it's protected or it's too rough for people." Again like the pikas, the populations that seemed to vanish were those on lower-elevation mountain ranges. In the last century, that part of California has had a 20 percent decrease in precipitation and a 1°C increase in temperature. Although the sheep are desert adapted, they too have limits to the amount of heat and dryness they can tolerate, Epps says. "They don't have a lot of margin out there."

"This looks like climate change has had an effect," he says. To see whether the remaining populations were vulnerable to extinction under various climate change scenarios, he and his colleagues ran some computer models. The models indicate that sheep populations on lower-elevation mountains are

at higher risk for extinction. When Epps resurveyed the
Sacramento Mountains sheep population, one that the models
predicted that is vulnerable to extinction, he found only two
males. Without females, the population is "functionally
extinct," he says. "It's a sad validation of the model."

Some organisms can—and do—shift north. Butterflies,
to name a few. Both in the western United States and in
Europe, various species of butterflies are expanding their
ranges northward. In 1999, Camille Parmesan, an ecologist at
the University of Texas–Austin, and her colleagues published a
paper in *Nature* showing that for 57 species of European butterflies, two-thirds had moved their ranges as far as 240
kilometers farther north in the 20th century.

These individual examples are all part of a larger trend,
say biologists. To demonstrate that, two teams of
researchers, one led by Parmesan and the other by Stanford
University ornithologist Terry Root, reviewed and analyzed
studies on various biotic changes that might be caused by
global warming. For more than 1,700 species from around
the globe, more than 80 percent had exhibited range
changes, phenological changes, or even some behavioral,
physiological, or genetic changes of the type expected if
warming temperatures were the cause.

Forecasting Future Extinctions

If the predictions of future warming are correct, what else will
happen in the biological world?

Scientists have long used a technique called bioclimatic
envelope modeling to indicate, based on an organism's known
climactic requirements, where geographically a particular

plant or animal could live. For many parts of the world, the climactic regime is much better known than the biota. So knowing a species' "bioclimatic envelope" can help biologists pinpoint where to look for a particular organism.

The rain forests of northeastern Australia have been designated a World Heritage site by UNESCO (United Nations Educational, Scientific and Cultural Organization) because of the region's rich biodiversity. Stephen E. Williams used bioclimatic envelope modeling to map where rain forest vertebrates might be found. Williams, an ecologist at the Cooperate Research Centre for Tropical Rainforest Ecology at James Cook University in Townsville, Australia, then applied the model to 65 species to see where they could live if warming increased by 1.4°C to 5.8°C, the amount predicted by the IPCC by 2100.

"Basically the results were so catastrophic and frightening that it completely changed the direction of the research," Williams says. "The predictions were that we were going to lose half of our endemic species, and the rest would be reduced to very small areas. As a conservation biologist, you think, well, the other things you're working on are not very important compared to this."

One tropical forest species, Costa Rica's golden toad, has already gone extinct because of climate change. If the climate continues to warm, Williams says, similar extinctions are likely in this part of the world also. His study includes 24 endemic species of birds, frogs, mammals and reptiles that, like the golden toad, are restricted to the tops of mountains. He says, "They're the most threatened by climate change. They've got absolutely nowhere to go—they're already sitting perched on the tops of these mountains. It only takes a couple of degrees' change in temperature to push their environment off the top of the mountain."

Other animals may not be resilient to the increased variability that climate change predicts. The green ringtail possum, another rain forest denizen, doesn't seem to cope well if temperature go above 30°C for more than several hours, according to Williams's colleague Andrew Krockenberger, an ecophysiologist at James Cook University in Cairns. Right now the possum lives where the hottest week of the year might reach 30°C. If warming brings just a few more heat waves, the possum could be in trouble.

It's not just the endemic species of Australian and Costa Rican mountains that will be threatened with extinction if the globe warms. Other researchers have constructed models similar to Williams's for biota of Europe, South Africa, Brazil, and Mexico. By looking at all the models together, ecologist Chris D. Thomas and his colleagues made extinction predictions for 1,103 species of plants, mammals, birds, amphibians, reptiles, and invertebrates throughout the world.

Thomas, now at the University of York, says of the worldwide extinction predictions, "They are grim—and we were surprised they ended up as large as they did."

The researchers took their collection of bioclimatic envelope models and applied various climate change predictions. Then the scientists added a wrinkle: They ran one set of models that assumed the organisms could move to wherever their new climate envelope ended up, and another model assuming the organisms were unable to migrate. The team then asked how many of the 1,103 species would be on death row by the year 2050.

Even in the best-case scenario, in which migration is possible, 18 percent of the species would be on the road to extinction by 2050. And, at worst, 35 percent would be among the doomed by 2050. Thomas says, "For some animals and plants with fairly long generations, it could be a very long time indeed before the last individuals die out." So, although in some cases individuals might hang on past the year 2050, the species would still die out.

Most climate change between now and 2050 is inevitable, Thomas says. "In doing the analysis, we imagined the situation frozen at 2050 conditions, bit in fact the situation is much worse than that," adding that most climate models predict as much additional warming between 2050 and 2100 as between now and 2050. "The high-end numbers are extremely scary . . . One imagines there would be fairly serious problems in a lot of biological systems if you're losing such high proportions of species."

In terms of counteracting the threat, Thomas hopes the team's work will spur some political action to reduce greenhouse emissions. "The primary thing to do is to minimize the amount of climate warming that takes place. That dwarfs everything else." Climate change, the team writes in their January 2004 *Nature* paper, should be ranked as a major, if not the greatest, threat to biodiversity worldwide.

Even before the devastating Southeast Asian tsunami of 2004 and the damage from Hurricane Katrina to America's Gulf

Coast region in 2005, many scientists warned that weather events around the globe were likely to worsen as a result of global warming. Still, some scientists challenge these theories and claim that the increase in deaths and material losses from hurricanes, tidal waves, and flooding are due to rising human populations, especially in highly susceptible coastal areas. Finally, in 2004, New York Times science writer Andrew C. Revkin's new study, published in the Journal of Climate, indicated that the warnings were indeed accurate. —RC

"Global Warming Is Expected to Raise Hurricane Intensity"
by Andrew C. Revkin
New York Times, September 30, 2004

Global warming is likely to produce a significant increase in the intensity and rainfall of hurricanes in coming decades, according to the most comprehensive computer analysis done so far.

By the 2080's, seas warmed by rising atmospheric concentrations of heat-trapping greenhouse gases could cause a typical hurricane to intensify about an extra half step on the five-step scale of destructive power, says the study, done on supercomputers at the Commerce Department's Geophysical Fluid Dynamics Laboratory in Princeton, N.J. And rainfall up to 60 miles from the core would be nearly 20 percent more intense.

Other computer modeling efforts have also predicted that hurricanes will grow stronger and wetter as a result of global warming. But this study is particularly significant, independent experts said, because it used half a dozen computer simulations of global climate, devised by separate groups at institutions around the world. The long-term trends it identifies are independent of the normal lulls and surges in hurricane activity that have been on display in recent decades.

The study was published online on Tuesday by *The Journal of Climate* and can be found at [http://www.gfdl.noaa.gov/reference/bibliography/2004/tk0401.pdf].

The new study of hurricanes and warming "is by far and away the most comprehensive effort" to assess the question using powerful computer simulations, said Dr. Kerry A. Emanuel, a hurricane expert at the Massachusetts Institute of Technology who has seen the paper but did not work on it. About the link between the warming of tropical oceans and storm intensity, he said, "This clinches the issue."

Dr. Emanuel and the study's authors cautioned that it was too soon to know whether hurricanes would form more or less frequently in a warmer world. Even as seas warm, for example, accelerating high-level winds can shred the towering cloud formations of a tropical storm.

But the authors said that even if the number of storms simply stayed the same, the increased intensity would substantially increase their potential for destruction.

Experts also said that rising sea levels caused by global warming would lead to more flooding from hurricanes—a point underlined at the United Nations this week by leaders of several small island nations, who pleaded for more attention to the potential for devastation from tidal surges.

The new study used four climate centers' mathematical approximations of the physics by which ocean heat fuels tropical storms.

With almost every combination of greenhouse-warmed oceans and atmosphere and formulas for storm dynamics, the results were the same: more powerful storms and more rainfall, said Robert Tuleya, one of the paper's two authors. He is a hurricane expert who recently retired after 31 years at the fluid dynamics laboratory and teaches at Old Dominion University in Norfolk, Va. The other author was Dr. Thomas R. Knutson of the Princeton laboratory.

Altogether, the researchers spawned around 1,300 virtual hurricanes using a more powerful version of the same super-computer simulations that generates Commerce Department forecasts of the tracks and behavior of real hurricanes.

Dr. James B. Elsner, a hurricane expert at Florida State University who was among the first to predict the recent surge in Atlantic storm activity, said the new study was a significant step in examining the impacts of a warmer future.

But like Dr. Emanuel, he also emphasized that the extraordinary complexity of the oceans and atmosphere made any scientific progress "baby steps toward a final answer."

CHAPTER THREE

PRODUCTION, DISTRIBUTION, AND CONSUMPTION: HOW CLIMATE CHANGE MAY ALTER AGRICULTURE AND INDUSTRY

While archaeological research has led to the conclusion that today's climate has been the key to successful crops, an increase in global temperatures would likely have the opposite effect, causing unpredictable weather and significant drops in crop yields. According to recent studies by experts at the National Aeronautics and Space Administration (NASA), the U.S. Department of Agriculture, and the Goddard Institute for Space Studies at Columbia University, rising temperatures are causing a variety of changes to global weather patterns that will worsen as temperatures increase, particularly in Southeast Asian countries. But the threat to farmers' livelihoods does not end with a potential increase in droughts. They will also experience severe storms, flooding, and changes to growing patterns. In addition, longer periods of warmer weather bring with them blight and a higher incidence of crop pests. According to writer Brian Halweil, there are a few solutions that farmers may find useful in the coming years, but ultimately, he urges

*people to consume local foods, a practice long believed to
reduce the energy needed to produce and transport food
around the country and the world. —RC*

"The Irony of Climate"
by Brian Halweil
WorldWatch, **March/April 2005**

High in the Peruvian Andes, a new disease has invaded the
potato fields in the town of Chacllabamba. Warmer and wetter weather associated with global climate change has
allowed late blight—the same fungus that caused the Irish
potato famine—to creep 4,000 meters up the mountainside
for the first time since humans started growing potatoes here
thousands of years ago. In 2003, Chacllabamba farmers saw
their crop of native potatoes almost totally destroyed.
Breeders are rushing to develop tubers resistant to the "new"
disease that retain the taste, texture, and quality preferred
by Andean populations.

Meanwhile, old-timers in Holmes County, Kansas, have
been struggling to tell which way the wind is blowing, so to
speak. On the one hand, the summers and winters are both
warmer, which means less snow and less snowmelt in the
spring and less water stored in the fields. On the other hand,
there's more rain, but it's falling in the early spring, rather than
during the summer growing season. So the crops might be
parched when they need water most. According to state climatologists, it's too early to say exactly how these changes will
play out—if farmers will be able to push their corn and wheat
fields onto formerly barren land or if the higher temperatures
will help once again to turn the grain fields of Kansas into a

dust bowl. Whatever happens, it's going to surprise the current generation of farmers.

Asian farmers, too, are facing their own climate-related problems. In the unirrigated rice paddies and wheat fields of Asia, the annual monsoon can make or break millions of lives. Yet the reliability of the monsoon is increasingly in doubt. For instance, El Niño events (the cyclical warming of surface waters in the eastern Pacific Ocean) often correspond with weaker monsoons, and El Niños will likely increase with global warming. During the El Niño–induced drought in 1997, Indonesian rice farmers pumped water from swamps close to their fields, but food losses were still high: 55 percent for dry-land maize and 41 percent for wetland maize, 34 percent for wetland rice, and 19 percent for cassava. The 1997 drought was followed by a particularly wet winter that delayed planting for two months in many areas and triggered heavy locust and rat infestations. According to Bambang Irawan of the Indonesian Center for Agricultural Socio-Economic Research and Development, in Bogor, this succession of poor harvests forced many families to eat less rice and turn to the less nutritious alternative of dried cassava. Some farmers sold off their jewelry and livestock, worked off the farm, or borrowed money to purchase rice, Irawan says. The prospects are for more of the same: "If we get a substantial global warming, there is no doubt in my mind that there will be serious changes to the monsoon," says David Rhind, a senior climate researcher with NASA's Goddard Institute for Space Studies.

Archaeologists believe that the shift to a warmer, wetter, and more stable climate at the end of the last ice age was key for humanity's successful foray into food production. Yet, from the American breadbasket to the North China Plain to the fields of southern Africa, farmers and climate scientists are finding that generations-old patterns of rainfall and temperature are shifting. Farming may be the human endeavor most dependent on a stable climate—and the industry that will struggle most to cope with more erratic weather, severe storms, and shifts in growing season lengths. While some optimists are predicting longer growing seasons and more abundant harvests as the climate warms, farmers are mostly reaping surprises.

Toward the Unknown (Climate) Region

For two decades, Hartwell Allen, a researcher with the University of Florida in Gainesville and the U.S. Department of Agriculture, has been growing rice, soybeans, and peanuts in plastic, greenhouse-like growth chambers that allow him to play God. He can control—"rather precisely"—the temperature, humidity, and levels of atmospheric carbon. "We grow the plants under a daily maximum/minimum cyclic temperature that would mimic the real world cycle," Allen says. His lab has tried regimes of 28 degrees C day/18 degrees C night, 32/22, 36/26, 40/30, and 44/34. "We ran one experiment to 48/38, and got very few surviving plants," he says. Allen found that while a doubling of carbon dioxide and a slightly increased temperature stimulate seeds to germinate and the plants to grow larger and lusher, the higher temperatures are deadly when the plant starts producing pollen. Every stage of the process—pollen transfer, the growth of the tube that links the pollen to the seed, the viability of the pollen itself—is highly sensitive. "It's all or nothing, if pollination isn't successful," Allen notes. At temperatures above 36 degrees C during pollination, peanut yields dropped about six percent per degree of temperature increase. Allen is particularly concerned about the implications for places like India and West Africa, where peanuts are a dietary staple and temperatures during the growing season are already well above 32 degrees C: "In these regions the crops are mostly rain-fed. If global warming also leads to drought in these areas, yields could be even lower."

As plant scientists refine their understanding of climate change and the subtle ways in which plants respond, they are beginning to think that the most serious threats to agriculture will not be the most dramatic: the lethal heatwave or severe drought or endless deluge. Instead, for plants that humans have bred to thrive in specific climactic conditions, it is those subtle shifts in temperatures and rainfall during key periods in the crops' lifecycles that will be most disruptive. Even today, crop losses associated with background climate variability are significantly higher than those caused by disasters such as hurricanes or flooding.

John Sheehy at the International Rice Research Institute in Manila has found that damage to the world's major grain crops begins when temperatures climb above 30 degrees C during flowering. At about 40 degrees C, yields are reduced to zero. "In rice, wheat, and maize, grain yields are likely to decline by 10 percent for every 1 degree C increase over 30 degrees. We are already at or close to this threshold," Sheehy says, noting regular heat damage in Cambodia, India, and his own center in the Philippines, where the average temperature is now 2.5 degrees C higher than 50 years ago. In particular, higher night-time temperatures forced the plants to work harder at respiration and thus sapped their energy, leaving less for producing grain. Sheehy estimates that grain yields in the tropics might fall as much as 30 percent over the next 50 years, during a period when the region's already malnourished population is projected to increase by 44 percent. (Sheehy and his colleagues think a potential solution is breeding rice and other crops to flower early in the morning or at night so that the sensitive temperature process misses the hottest part of the day. But, he says, "we haven't been successful in getting any real funds for the work.") The world's major plants can cope with temperature shifts to some extent, but since the dawn of agriculture farmers have selected plants that thrive in stable conditions.

Climatologists consulting their computer climate models see anything but stability, however. As greenhouse gases trap more of the sun's heat in the Earth's atmosphere, there is also more energy in the climate system, which means more extreme swings—dry to wet, hot to cold. (This is the reason that there can still be severe winters on a warming planet, or that March 2004 was the third-warmest month on record after one of the coldest winters ever.) Among those projected impacts that climatologists have already observed in most regions: higher maximum temperatures and more hot days, higher minimum temperatures and fewer cold days, more variable and extreme rainfall events, and increased summer drying and associated risk of drought in continental interiors. All of these conditions will likely accelerate into the next century.

Cynthia Rosenzweig, a senior research scholar with the Goddard Institute for Space Studies at Columbia University, argues that although the climate models will always be improving, there are certain changes we can already predict with a level of confidence. First, most studies indicate "intensification of the hydrological cycle," which essentially means more droughts and floods, and more variable and extreme rainfall.

Second, Rosenzweig says, "basically every study has shown that there will be increased incidence of crop pests." Longer growing seasons mean more generations of pests during the summer, while shorter and warmer winters mean that fewer adults, larvae, and eggs will die off.

Third, most climatologists agree that climate change will hit farmers in the developing world hardest. This is partly a result of geography. Farmers in the tropics already find themselves near the temperature limits for most major crops, so any warming is likely to push their crops over the top. "All increases in temperature, however small, will lead to decreases in production," says Robert Watson, chief scientist at the World Bank and former chairman of the Intergovernmental Panel on Climate Change. "Studies have consistently shown that agricultural regions in the developing world are more vulnerable, even before we consider the ability to cope," because of poverty, more limited irrigation technology, and lack of weather tracking systems. "Look at the coping strategies, and then it's a real double whammy," Rosenzweig says. In sub-Saharan Africa—ground zero of global hunger, where the number of starving people has doubled in the last 20 years—the current situation will undoubtedly be exacerbated by the climate crisis. (And by the 2080s, Watson says, projections indicate that even temperate latitudes will begin to approach the upper limit of the productive temperature range.)

Coping with Change

"Scientists may indeed need decades to be sure that climate change is taking place," says Patrick Luganda, chairman of the Network of Climate Journalists in the Greater Horn of Africa. "But, on the ground, farmers have no choice but to deal with the daily reality as best they can." Luganda says that several years ago local farming communities in Uganda could determine the onset of rains and their cessation with a fair amount of accuracy. "These days there is no guarantee that the long rains will start, or stop, at the usual time," Luganda says. The Ateso people in north-central Uganda report the disappearance of asisinit, a swamp grass favored for thatch houses because of its beauty and durability. The grass is increasingly rare because farmers have started to plant rice and millet in swampy areas in response to more frequent droughts. (Rice farmers in Indonesia coping with droughts have done the same.) Farmers have also begun to sow a wider diversity of crops and to stagger their plantings to hedge against abrupt climate shifts. Luganda adds that repeated crop failures have pushed many farmers into the urban centers: the final coping mechanism.

The many variables associated with climate change make coping difficult, but hardly futile. In some cases, farmers may need to install sprinklers to help them survive more droughts. In other cases, plant breeders will need to look for crop varieties that can withstand a greater range of temperatures. The good news is that many of the same changes that will help farmers cope with climate change will also make communities more self-sufficient and reduce dependence on the long-distance food chain.

Planting a wider range of crops, for instance, is perhaps farmers' best hedge against more erratic weather. In parts of Africa, planting trees alongside crops—a system called agroforestry that might include shade coffee and cacao, or leguminous trees with corn—might be part of the answer. "There is good reason to believe that these systems will be more resilient than a maize monoculture," says Lou Verchot, the lead scientist on climate change at the International Centre for Research in Agroforestry in Nairobi. The trees send their roots considerably deeper than the crops, allowing them to survive a drought that might damage the grain crop. The tree roots will also pump water into the upper soil layers where crops can tap it. Trees improve the soil as well: their roots create spaces for water flow and their leaves decompose into compost. In other words, a farmer who has trees won't lose everything. Farmers in central Kenya are using a mix of coffee, macadamia nuts, and cereals that results in as many as three marketable crops in a good year. "Of course, in any one year, the monoculture will yield more money," Verchot admits, "but farmers need to work on many years." These diverse crop mixes are all the more relevant since rising temperatures will eliminate much of the traditional coffee- and tea-growing areas in the Caribbean, Latin America, and Africa. In Uganda, where coffee and tea account for nearly 100 percent of agricultural exports, an average temperature rise of 2 degrees C would dramatically reduce the harvest, as all but the highest altitude areas become too hot to grow coffee.

In essence, farms will best resist a wide range of shocks by making themselves more diverse and less dependent on outside inputs. A farmer growing a single variety of wheat is more likely to lose the whole crop when the temperature shifts dramatically than a farmer growing several wheat varieties, or better yet, several varieties of plants besides wheat. The additional crops help form a sort of ecological bulwark against blows from climate change. "It will be important to devise more resilient agricultural production systems that can absorb and survive more variability," argues Fred Kirschenmann, director of the Leopold Center for Sustainable Agriculture at Iowa State University. At his own family farm in North Dakota, Kirschenmann has struggled with two years of abnormal weather that nearly eliminated one crop and devastated another. Diversified farms will cope better with drought, increased pests, and a range of other climate-related jolts. And they will tend to be less reliant on fertilizers and pesticides, and the fossil fuel inputs they require. Climate change might also be the best argument for preserving local crop varieties around the world, so that plant breeders can draw from as wide a palette as possible when trying to develop plants that can cope with more frequent drought or new pests.

Farms with trees planted strategically between crops will not only better withstand torrential downpours and parching droughts, they will also "lock up" more carbon. Lou Verchot says that the improved fallows used in Africa can lock up 10–20 times the carbon of nearby cereal monocultures, and 30 percent of the carbon in an intact forest. And building up a soil's stock of organic matter—the dark, spongy stuff in soils that stores carbon and gives them their rich smell—not only increases the amount of water the soil can hold (good for weathering droughts), but also helps bind more nutrients (good for crop growth).

Best of all, for farmers at least, systems that store more carbon are often considerably more profitable, and they might become even more so if farmers get paid to store carbon under the Kyoto Protocol. There is a plan, for instance, to pay farmers in Chiapas, Mexico, to shift from farming that involves regular forest clearing to agroforestry. The International Automobile

Federation is funding the project as part of its commitment to reducing carbon emissions from sponsored sports car races. Not only that, "increased costs for fossil fuels will accelerate demand for renewable energies," says Mark Muller of the Institute for Agriculture and Trade Policy in Minneapolis, Minnesota, who believes that farmers will find new markets for biomass fuels like switchgrass that can be grown on the farm, as well as additional royalties from installing wind turbines on their farms.

However, "carbon farming is a temporary solution," according to Marty Bender of the Land Institute's Sunshine Farm in Salina, Kansas. He points to a recent paper in *Science* showing that even if America's soils were returned to their pre-plow carbon content—a theoretical maximum for how much carbon they could lock up—this would be equal to only two decades of American carbon emissions. "That is how little time we will be buying," Bender says, "despite the fact that it may take a hundred years of aggressive, national carbon farming and forestry to restore this lost carbon." (Cynthia Rosenzweig also notes that the potential to lock up carbon is limited, and that a warmer planet will reduce the amount of carbon that soils can hold: as land heats up, invigorated soil microbes respire more carbon dioxide.)

"We really should be focusing on energy efficiency and energy conservation to reduce the carbon emissions by our national economy," Bender concludes. That's why Sunshine Farm, which Bender directs, has been farming without fossil fuels, fertilizers, or pesticides in order to reduce its contribution to climate change and to find an inherently local solution to a global problem. As the name implies, Sunshine Farm runs essentially on sunlight. Homegrown sunflower seeds and soybeans become biodiesel that fuels tractors and trucks. The farm raises nearly three-fourths of the feed—oats, grain sorghum, and alfalfa—for its draft horses, beef cattle, and poultry. Manure and legumes in the crop rotation substitute for energy-gobbling nitrogen fertilizers. A 4.5-kilowatt photovoltaic array powers the workshop tools, electric fencing, water pumps, and chick brooding pens. The farm has eliminated an amount of energy equivalent to that used to make and transport 90 percent of its supplies. (Including the energy required to make the farm's machinery lowers the figure to 50 percent, still a huge gain over the standard American farm.)

But these energy savings are only part of this distinctly local solution to an undeniably global problem, Bender says. "If local food systems could eliminate the need for half of the energy used for food processing and distribution, then that would save 30 percent of the fossil energy used in the U.S. food system," Bender reasons. "Considering that local foods will require some energy use, let's round the net savings down to 25 percent. In comparison, on-farm direct and indirect energy consumption constitutes 20 percent of energy use in the U.S. food system. Hence, local food systems could potentially save more energy than is used on American farms."

In other words, as climate tremors disrupt the vast intercontinental web of food production and rearrange the world's major breadbaskets, depending on food from distant suppliers will be more expensive and more precarious. It will be cheaper and easier to cope with local weather shifts, and with more limited supplies of fossil fuels, than to ship in a commodity from afar.

Agriculture is in third place, far behind energy use and chlorofluorocarbon production, as a contributor to climate warming. For farms to play a significant role, changes in cropping practices must happen on a large scale, across large swaths of India and Brazil and China and the American Midwest. As Bender suggests, farmers will be able to shore up their defenses against climate change, and can make obvious reductions in their own energy use which could save them money.

But the lasting solution to greenhouse gas emissions and climate change will depend mostly on the choices that everyone else makes. According to the London-based NGO Safe Alliance, a basic meal—some meat, grain, fruits, and vegetables—using imported ingredients can easily generate four times the greenhouse gas emissions as the same meal with ingredients from local sources. In terms of our personal contribution to climate change, eating local can be as important as driving a fuel-efficient car, or giving up the car for a bike. As politicians struggle to muster the will power to confront the climate crisis, ensuring that farmers have a less erratic climate in which to raise the world's food shouldn't be too hard a sell.

While environmentalists have long been opposed to nuclear power plants, citing dangers such as improper disposal of nuclear waste and the potential for the accidental release of nuclear material, Science *writer Richard A. Meserve urges environmentalists concerned about global warming to reconsider nuclear power as a cleaner source of energy than*

fossil fuels. A recent study released by the Massachusetts Institute of Technology confirms Americans' reluctance; the study also revealed that nuclear power plants should be maintained as a viable energy option for the future, especially as the world taps into its dwindling supplies of oil and natural gas. —RC

"Global Warming and Nuclear Power"
by Richard A. Meserve
Science, January 23, 2004

A recent Massachusetts Institute of Technology (MIT) study on the future of nuclear power argues that nuclear power should be maintained as an energy option because it is an important carbon-free source of power that can potentially make a significant contribution to future electricity supply. [S. Ansolabehere, et. al, *The Future of Nuclear Power: An Interdisciplinary MIT Study*, Massachusetts Institute of Technology, Cambridge, MA, 2003.] Unfortunately, the study also observes, based on a survey of adults in the United States, that those who are very concerned about global warming are no more likely to support nuclear power than those who are not. Other evidence suggests that the responses in Europe would not be very different. As a result, the MIT authors conclude that public education may be needed to broaden understanding of the links among global warming, fossil fuel usage, and the need for low-carbon energy sources.

For those who are concerned about our future climate, the survey should be disturbing. A realistic response to global warming should involve harnessing a variety of energy options: increased use of renewable energy sources, sequestration of carbon at fossil-fuel plants, enhanced efficiency in energy generation and use, and increased reliance on nuclear power. Because public misunderstanding is likely to manifest itself in the political arena, greater appreciation of the relation between nuclear power and emissions reduction may be essential if use of the nuclear option is to be significantly expanded.

Unfortunately, two institutions that might be expected to explain the facts are largely silent on this issue. Environmental groups include a large and dedicated antinuclear constituency, so even environmentalists who might give nuclear a second look might hesitate to embrace that view publicly. The nuclear industry is reluctant to advance the case because generating companies also rely on fossil-fuel plants (primarily using carbon-intensive coal) for electricity production. This sector thus has a strong disincentive to use global warming as a justification for nuclear power because of the implication of that argument for other components of the companies' supply portfolios.

As for the Bush administration, it has aggressively supported nuclear power but has carefully avoided emphasizing the link between nuclear power and the global climate's response to increasing concentrations of greenhouse gases. This no doubt reflects the hesitancy that has characterized the administration's approach to the global warming issue.

We thus confront a paradoxical situation. Those who should be the strongest advocates of nuclear power—environmentalists, governmental policy-makers concerned about global warming, and generating companies with an economic stake in nuclear's future—are unable or unwilling to advance the most compelling argument in support of it. Without advocacy by those who see the benefits of nuclear power, it is only to be expected that full exploitation of the nuclear option will be limited or deferred indefinitely.

Of course, any support for nuclear power should recognize the challenges it presents. Nuclear power is unacceptable unless operators are committed to safe operations and the Nuclear Regulatory Commission exercises careful and detailed oversight. Continuing progress toward the safe final disposition of nuclear waste must be demanded. And tightening safeguards against the diversion of commercial technology to weapons use deserves to be given a high priority around the globe.

Fortunately, all of these challenges can be met. Nuclear power plants have better safety performance today than ever, and future generations of reactors will have design modifications that enhance safety even further. Although debate continues about whether Yucca Mountain is an appropriate disposal site for nuclear waste, the scientific community is in agreement that deep geological disposal somewhere will be a satisfactory means for the disposition of spent fuel. And strengthened international institutions and commitments hold the promise of preventing nuclear power from contributing to the proliferation of nuclear weapons.

For those who are serious about confronting global warming, nuclear power should be seen as part of the solution. Although it is unlikely that many environmental groups will become enthusiastic proponents of nuclear power, the harsh reality is that any serious program to address global warming cannot afford to jettison any technology prematurely. Careful weighing of the risks supports the conclusion that nuclear power at the least must be a bridging technology until other carbon-free energy options become more readily available. The stakes are large, and the scientific and educational community should seek to ensure that the public understands the critical link between nuclear power and climate change.

In this comprehensive examination of the world's current energy usage and the potential effects of global warming, Foreign Affairs *writers S. Julio Friedmann and Thomas Homer-Dixon explore the effects of rising CO_2 levels, the future of renewable energy, and a rather unique solution to reducing carbon levels: geologic carbon sequestration. By using this method of depositing and storing carbon underground where it cannot harm the atmosphere, scientists believe they can help reduce, or at least lessen the effects of rising temperatures. Overall, Friedmann and Homer-Dixon express the drastic need of world leaders to take seriously the extensive research, development, and financial support that will be required by the public and private sector to meet the energy demands of a growing population and a changing world. —RC*

From "Out of the Energy Box"
by S. Julio Friedmann and Thomas Homer-Dixon
Foreign Affairs, **November/December 2004**

Only Richard Nixon could go to China. And maybe only oil industry CEOs can lead action on global climate change. Lord Browne, the head of BP, has stated in no uncertain terms that climate change is real, and he has made it BP's responsibility to cut down on the greenhouse-gas emissions that are upsetting the earth's climate.

The prognosis for the future of climate change is indeed alarming. Scientists say plausible scenarios include terrible droughts, crop failures, and dying forests around the Mediterranean and in the United States, South America, India, China, and Africa. Sea levels are expected to rise significantly, drowning islands and possibly displacing hundreds of millions of people from coastlines, where more than a third of the world's population lives. Ground water supplies are set to shrink, reservoirs to dry up. Wildfires and violent storms will strike more often and much harder. And much of this change is expected within the next 50 years.

Most scientists believe that recent global warming is largely the result of human energy consumption, which releases carbon dioxide, a powerful greenhouse gas, into the atmosphere. Massive, almost inconceivable amounts of energy are used to do everything these days, from building airplanes to running sewer systems and hospital equipment. Energy is the essence of modern civilization, and as societies and economies grow, so does their energy consumption.

In the United States and most other developed countries, 85 percent of this energy comes from fossil fuels (mainly coal, oil, and natural gas). In developing countries, wood, charcoal, straw, and cow dung still meet a large portion of heating and cooking needs, but the shift to fossil fuels is happening fast. Global energy consumption is growing at roughly two percent per year and is projected to double by 2035 and triple by 2055 . . .

Reducing the consumption of energy and increasing its efficient use would help control emissions. But such measures will not likely be sufficient to solve the problem. Nor will replacing fossil fuels with alternative sources of energy, which remain prohibitively expensive or too impractical to be used on a large scale. Modern economies are thus bound to remain dependent on carbon dioxide-releasing fuels for the foreseeable future.

Although energy needs and environmental constraints have created this tight energy box, an important technology has emerged that offers a way out of it, at least temporarily. Called "carbon sequestration," it is a way to store carbon dioxide in a benign form and in a safe place, allowing the continued use of fossil fuels without the dreadful effects of climate change. With the right economic incentives and regulatory framework, moreover, sequestration can be made attractive to investors and so developed more widely. And it should be, because the technology may be the only realistic way to satisfy the world's gargantuan energy needs while responsibly mitigating their side effects. As Lord Oxburgh, the Chairman of the British arm of the Royal Dutch/Shell group, said recently, "sequestration is difficult: But if we don't have [it], I see very little hope for the world."

Insufficient Efficiency

The world's energy needs—and their potential effects on the environment—can hardly be exaggerated. Producing, processing, and transporting energy costs more than $3.5 trillion every year more than the U.S. federal budget or the GDP of most nations. The expense increases significantly every year, as the world's population and economy grow.

Consider the energy needs of the United States, home to less than one-twentieth of the world's population but which produces about a quarter of its carbon dioxide emissions. U.S. energy consumption now reaches 97.6 quadrillion British thermal units (quads), and it is expected to grow by at least another 95 quads over the next 50 years. Assuming these new needs were to be covered by nuclear power, which provides a lot of electricity without emitting carbon dioxide, one would have to build 1,500 nuclear plants to supplement today's 104 facilities a new plant about every 10 days—to meet projected demand. Even if such a plan were possible, it would do nothing to reduce carbon dioxide emissions; it would only help keep them at today's already very high levels.

These staggering requirements mean that simply conserving energy and using it more efficiently cannot solve the problem. Although the United States has grown much more efficient over the past two decades, it still has not reduced its carbon emissions. Despite total efficiency gains of over 35 percent since 1980, annual use in the United States soared from 78 quads to nearly 100 quads between 1980 and 2000, and annual carbon emissions from 1,288 to 1,562 million metric tons. Why the disparity? Because although efficiency has improved on average by almost two percent annually over the last 20 years, GDP has grown at over three percent annually.

Moreover, even at that rate, efficiency cannot improve indefinitely, because manufacturers and entrepreneurs exploit the easiest ways of saving energy first, and so it may be harder and more expensive to achieve more gains. Even if that were not so, carbon emission rates would not drop unless economic growth dropped even more. And no economic policymaker—certainly no politician—would settle for a growth rate of less than two percent, when that level is too low even to absorb new labor entering the work force.

Strict conservation policies are even less feasible for the developing world, which sees poverty as its chief problem and is trying to grow as fast as possible. China grew at 9.1 percent in 2003, and the country's phenomenal appetite for steel, aluminum, copper, and cement caused its fossil fuel consumption to surge—turning it into the world's second-largest petroleum importer after the United States. Chinese leaders have made it clear that they want a billion cars for their billion potential drivers. But they cannot achieve a Western standard of living without also drastically increasing energy consumption and carbon dioxide emissions. In fact, current projections show that by 2020 China will overtake the United States as the world's leading carbon dioxide emitter.

Poor Substitutes

With rising energy needs and volatile oil prices, some advanced economies have started to look for alternatives to conventional coal and petroleum. But substitution is only a partial solution. Making most electricity from pulverized coal, natural gas, nuclear power, or solar energy is either problematic or too costly.

Coal is a versatile, high-energy fuel that is plentiful, cheap, and easily transported. It is also very dirty. Burning coal creates a lot of carbon dioxide—much more, per unit of energy produced, than burning any other fossil fuel. It also releases mercury, particulates, and sulfur dioxide (which causes acid rain), and extracting coal is harmful to both the environment and workers, who often suffer accidents in mines or contract black-lung disease.

Natural gas (or methane), which burns cleanly, with small emissions of carbon dioxide and even smaller emissions of other pollutants, has become a preferred energy source for many countries. It too is abundant around the planet: on land in Bolivia, the Middle East, Central Asia, and Siberia and offshore in the Arctic, the Gulf of Mexico, and along the western coast of Africa.

Unfortunately, most gas supplies lie far away from users, so transportation costs are high. The United States, once impervious to these concerns thanks to abundant resources at home and in Canada, has recently had to face problems caused by dwindling domestic supplies and increased demand. Although about 16,000 new gas wells were drilled in the lower 48 states in 2002, production declined by six percent and shortages caused the price of gas to spike to three times its base cost. In the past decade, moreover, the base cost of natural gas has almost doubled in the United States, causing many gas-powered plants to sit idle.

Energy experts have considered one solution: importing gas from far-flung suppliers by transporting it, in liquefied form, in ships fitted with high-pressure storage tanks. But right now the United States has only four terminals equipped to receive liquefied gas, which together accept only a quarter of a quad every year. Another 40 terminals are planned or proposed, but they would likely provide less than three quads in total. To meet demand, hundreds more would have to be built . . .

Nuclear power does not emit carbon dioxide either, and it has other advantages to boot. Nuclear plants can be built in large numbers close to the populations they serve, without risk of interrupted fuel supply. They can be designed to be "inherently safe," with an infinitesimally small risk of melt-down, and thanks to "breeder" technology, to produce their own fuel.

Yet nuclear power is almost twice as expensive as fossil-fuel energy; and, like liquefied gas, it presents serious security risks. Nuclear power plants, especially breeder reactors, pro-duce a lot of highly radioactive waste, chiefly plutonium . . . But such nuclear material . . . is extremely toxic, terrorists could use it for radiological or "dirty" bombs, and it contains plutonium, which can be extracted to make atomic weapons.

Sources of renewable energy, such as solar power, pose no such danger, but they are inherently ill-suited to modern energy needs. Many of the regions that consume the most energy do not have bright, year-round sunlight. (Think of New York City, London, Moscow, and Tokyo in the long fall and win-ter seasons.) Solar energy has a low power density, so even in regions where sunlight is steady and bright, as in the Mojave or Sahara deserts, a square meter receives little power every day. Industrial zones and high-density urban cores consume many times more power per square meter than they receive . . .

As a result, generating power from the sun requires huge amounts of land and money. Admittedly, the price of solar energy is falling, and optimists believe that it may be competi-tive with that of conventional energy within 10 to 20 years. But, for now, it remains expensive: about three to eight times more than coal or gas power. Satisfying current U.S. electrical consumption would require nearly 10 billion square meters of photovoltaic solar panels. At about $500 per square meter, the panels alone would cost $5 trillion, twice the U.S. federal budget for 2004 and nearly half of U.S. GDP. Connecting this

power to the main electrical grid and installing a means to
store it would double or triple the price tag.

Hydrogen is no panacea either. It is much touted for yield-
ing only heat and water—no carbon dioxide, acid rain, ozone, or
soot—when it is consumed. And, when used as a fuel for transportation, it is critical in helping reduce carbon dioxide
emissions. But because it is not a primary source of energy, it
has large-scale supply problems. Hydrogen cannot be extracted
like oil or coal. It can be made through electrolysis, by running
an electric current through water. But that process begs the
question: where does the electric current come from? If the
world had enough cheap, clean, emissions-free electricity to
make hydrogen, there would not be much need for making it at
all. In most industrial applications, hydrogen is made by combin-
ing steam with natural gas and then changing the mixture into
hydrogen. But that process emits carbon dioxide. So although
consuming hydrogen for energy does not pollute, making hydrogen this way in the first place does . . .

Although it is also possible to make hydrogen without
generating undesirable byproducts, those methods are not
economically viable yet. The United States could produce
hydrogen using electricity from solar or nuclear power. But
to replace the oil it uses for surface transportation would
require 230,000 tons of hydrogen every day (enough to fill
13,000 Hindenburg blimps). That, in turn, would require
nearly doubling the country's average electricity-generating
capacity and covering an area the size of Massachusetts with
solar panels—just to produce transportation fuel.

No other single source of energy offers a viable solution.
Wind energy, like solar energy, poses a power-density problem,

and it supplies power only intermittently: when the wind blows. Geothermal, fusion, and space-based solar power all face major hurdles due to cost, deployment, supply, or technology. There are few good locations left in the world to build large dams and generate power from water. Traditional biofuels (like biodiesel and ethanol), while neutral in terms of carbon dioxide emissions, have requirements relating to cost, land use, and water that limit their effectiveness at the scale required.

Taking Out the Trash

For the foreseeable future, then, the United States and the world must continue to rely on fossil fuels—and suffer their attendant climate-altering waste . . . [but] their harmful effects can be drastically limited.

First, it is important to recognize that greenhouse-gas emissions are a kind of trash. One hundred years ago, most people just chucked their garbage out the window, turning cities into rank concentrations of waste and sewage. Vastly more trash is generated now than then, but in most places it is removed and taken where rot, stench, and contamination can be contained.

Like trash, carbon dioxide can be sequestered. Trees and plants already do it: they absorb the gas and turn it into leaves, wood, and roots. But to make a dent in global warming, massive amounts of carbon need to be stored away for a long time—at least a few hundred years—and trees and plants are not up to the task.

That is where geologic carbon sequestration comes in. The technology; formally called "carbon capture and storage," returns the carbon dioxide to where it came from—underground—by injecting it into old oil or gas fields, unminable coalfields, or deep, briny aquifers (today's preferred storage site for toxic waste). Geologic storage requires deep, porous reservoirs covered by a layer of impermeable rock to prevent leakage. But preliminary estimates indicate that there is enough storage capacity close to today's major sources of carbon dioxide to hold many decades' worth of emissions safely, with a low chance of leakage or other risk to ecosystems or the public.

There are a few catches, of course. Only a highly concentrated stream of carbon dioxide can be stored, and it must be captured from retrofitted or brand-new power plants. The costs of upgrading or building such facilities are significant. But they are comparable to those of developing wind and nuclear power, and in many instances lower. Once a low-cost device to capture carbon dioxide from fossil-fuel streams is engineered, carbon sequestration will add only an incremental cost—roughly five to ten percent—to today's energy sources. The carbon dioxide of most of today's emitters, such as coal-fired power plants, could then be captured, lowering emissions dramatically without affecting energy consumption.

The technology is already available. The integrated gasified combined cycle (IGCC) coal-fired power plant crushes coal and mixes it with steam to make a hot combustible fluid called "syngas," stripping out sulfur, mercury, and other toxic pollutants. When syngas is consumed, it releases large amounts of electric power, hydrogen, and a stream of carbon dioxide suitable for capture and geologic storage. If the emissions are sequestered, the IGCC becomes a zero-emission plant (ZEP). Coal-power generation has never looked so sexy.

Even better, ZEPS based on gasification technology can burn a wide range of fuels besides coal. Waste biomass, such as corn residues, lawn clippings, and wood chips, and a gooey mixture of water and tar called "orimulsion" are suitable. Thus all could be used to generate both electricity and hydrogen.

The U.S. Department of Energy (DOE) thinks ZEPS can be economically viable. In February 2003, it announced plans to build and deploy the prototype FutureGen power plant. The FutureGen plant will be small, producing only 275 megawatts, but the project is worthwhile nonetheless, for it will validate the technology. Norway, Australia, Canada, and Germany are already developing ZEPS that burn coal, gas, and biomass; China and India, countries with huge populations, energy demands, and coal supplies, are considering the idea. Industry has also begun to invest heavily in the technology. In August 2004, American Electric Power announced plans to build a commercial IGCC before 2010. The plant will cost a lot upfront, but it has two benefits: very high efficiency and an emissions stream that can be captured and stored at low cost.

Given their considerable benefits, ZEPS must be central to any serious energy policy. By burning coal, orimulsion, bio-mass, and even garbage, ZEPS can provide enormous amounts of both electrical power and hydrogen while dramatically cutting greenhouse-gas emissions—all, if done right, without breaking the bank . . .

Getting Real

Although technology makes geologic sequestration possible, only the right incentives and regulations can make it viable. Curbing global warming takes motivated and ingenious scientists, engineers, and investors, as well as appropriate market and government institutions.

Creating a carbon dioxide commodity exchange would be a good start. If reducing greenhouse gas emissions has social value, it should be given a market value. People who take carbon dioxide from burning fossil fuels and sequester it underground, producing benefits for current and future generations, should be rewarded. So should investors who risk capital to build new electricity plants, pipelines, and storage reservoirs. To generate and allocate these rewards, sophisticated markets should be developed to assess the potential of carbon-storage ventures and return profits to people who launched them. The Chicago Climate Exchange, an embryonic carbon dioxide market, traded its first one million tons of carbon dioxide in June 2004 . . . and the Kyoto Protocol . . . [will] create a worldwide emissions market. Both are underpinned by a regulatory regime that caps emissions and allows countries, corporations, or other economic actors to trade emission credits. In the United States, a similar mechanism has significantly reduced acid rain, mercury pollution, and other byproducts of coal burning . . .

Rich industrial countries such as the United States, Canada, and members of the European Union must play a key role in the development and deployment of these technologies. Poor countries have little incentive to investigate expensive, low-emission energy sources when they face urgent economic needs. So rich countries should invest heavily in research and development (R&D) in all energy sectors, to promote conservation, develop cheap and versatile forms of renewable energy, and, above all, test the viability of large-scale geologic carbon sequestration.

Unfortunately, spending on energy research has dropped precipitously in all industrial countries except Japan. In real terms, combined industrial and governmental R&D in the energy sector has declined by more than 70 percent over the last 30 years. In Germany, spending has fallen even more, including for nuclear and wind research. The International Energy Agency (IEA) estimates that investments in excess of $200 billion are needed each year just to meet increased energy demand, let alone to investigate alternatives.

This alarming trend must be reversed in all industrialized countries. Specifically, nations should subsidize a diverse range of field experiments for geologic storage to show that the technology can be made both feasible and safe. Dedicated experimental facilities, not just more demonstration projects, are needed to establish the viability of sequestration.

To that end, the U.S. State Department, the DOE, and the relevant ministries from 16 nations formed the Carbon Sequestration Leadership Forum to discuss technical and policy issues relating to geologic storage and other forms of carbon sequestration. In June 2003, Australia, Brazil, Canada, China, India, Indonesia, Japan, Mexico, and many European nations signed a declaration stating their commitment to using carbon sequestration to lower global carbon dioxide emissions. In addition, the DOE has designated Teapot Dome (yes, that Teapot Dome) as an experimental facility for carbon storage and has launched a new storage experiment, the Frio Brine Pilot, in southern Texas.

Concentrations of greenhouse gases in the atmosphere cannot be stabilized at current levels. The most that can be done—if even that—is to stop the increase at about twice pre-industrial levels. This means capping carbon dioxide concentration at about 560 parts per million (PPM). (It is at 380 PPM today.) By itself, that concentration could be high enough to bring a Climactic and environmental catastrophe, but limiting it to even that level will require very clever technology and wise, concerted policy.

Nonetheless, the United States and other Western states should embrace this challenge as wholeheartedly and with the same dedication, investment, and smarts they once committed to containing the Soviet Union. Funding for key energy technologies should be increased a hundred fold to develop large-scale field demonstrations and sharply lower the cost of capturing carbon dioxide. Such projects should proceed as public-private partnerships, with strong government, university, and industrial leadership across many countries and an international emissions-trading framework designed to sustain economic growth. Incentives such as tax cuts should be provided to early actors, and multinational companies that reduce emissions abroad should be given credit in their home countries.

The G-8 group of highly industrialized nations should also hold energy and emissions summits in parallel with its annual economic meetings to consider technologies and policies that could be adopted by large developing countries. Industrial nations must also spearhead a crash, five-year survey of global geology to map the planet's subsurface capacity for storing carbon dioxide and so underpin cost predictions and support a carbon dioxide-trading regime. Australia has just completed such an effort, which required three years, dozens of scientists, and large-scale industrial collaboration. The United States, Canada, and other states have begun to set their geologic surveys to the task, but they should do much more. Meanwhile, they should increase efforts supporting energy efficiency, renewable energy, and nuclear fission, because only a wide portfolio of measures can ultimately be effective.

Storing greenhouse gases underground will require immense technological, infrastructural, and organizational changes. Such measures may seem formidable, but they should be treated as an incidental cost of maintaining energy-intensive economies, much like trash collection and disposal. Now is not the time for denial or avoidance; managing the damage caused by carbon dioxide emissions has become urgent. With every year that passes, the problem and the cost of fixing it become much greater—as does the chance that the damage already done is irreversible.

CHAPTER FOUR

SCIENCE, TECHNOLOGY, AND SOCIETY: WHAT WE KNOW NOW

This article addresses the gap between scientists who argue for immediate action to prevent or forestall the effects of global warming and those who claim the urgency surrounding climate change is too greatly amplified. Science writer Fred Pearce concludes that while we can all agree that Earth is indeed warming, this could be due to human activity or a change in solar cycles or both. There are a variety of factors that can influence the rate of temperature increase. Some of these factors include atmospheric insulators (such as volcanic ash and cloud cover), increases in water vapor, the exposure of granite in Arctic regions where glaciers are melting, and the drop in salinity due to rising sea levels. And while Pearce presents the information in a clear and rational summary, he leaves the final conclusion up to his readers. —RC

"Climate Change: Menace or Myth?"
by Fred Pearce
New Scientist, February 12, 2005

On 16 February, the Kyoto Protocol comes into force. Whether you see this as a triumph of international cooperation or a case of too little, too late, there is no doubt that it was only made possible by decades of dedicated work by climate scientists. Yet as these same researchers celebrate their most notable achievement, their work is being denigrated as never before.

The hostile criticism is coming from sceptics who question the reality of climate change. Critics have always been around, but in recent months their voices have become increasingly prominent and influential. One British newspaper called climate change a "global fraud" based on "left-wing, anti-American, anti-west ideology." A London-based think tank described the UK's chief scientific adviser, David King, as "an embarrassment" for believing that climate change is a bigger threat than terrorism. And the bestselling author Michael Crichton, in his much publicised new novel *State of Fear*, portrays global warming as an evil plot perpetuated by environmental extremists.

If the sceptics are to be believed, the evidence for global warming is full of holes and the field is riven with argument and uncertainty. The apparent scientific consensus over global warming only exists, they say, because it is enforced by scientific establishment riding the gravy train, aided and abetted by governments keen to play the politics of fear. It's easy to dismiss such claims as politically motivated and with no basis in fact—especially as the majority of sceptics are economists, business people or politicians, not scientists. But there are nagging doubts. Could the sceptics be onto something? Are we, after all, being taken for a ride?

This is perhaps the most crucial scientific question of the 21st century. The winning side in the climate debate will shape economic, political and technological developments for years, even centuries, to come. With so much at stake, it is crucial that the right side wins. But which side is right? What is the evidence that human activity is warming the world, and how reliable is it?

First, the basic physics. It is beyond doubt that certain gases in the atmosphere, most importantly water vapour and carbon dioxide, trap infrared radiation emitted by the Earth's surface and so have a greenhouse effect. This in itself is no bad thing. Indeed, without them the planet would freeze. There is also no doubt that human activity is pumping CO_2 into the atmosphere, and that this has caused a sustained year-on-year rise in CO_2 concentrations. For almost 60 years, measurements at the Mauna Loa observatory in Hawaii have charted this rise, and it is largely uncontested that today's concentrations are about 35 per cent above pre-industrial levels.

The effect this has on the planet is also measurable. In 2000, researchers based at Imperial College London examined satellite data covering almost three decades to plot changes in the amount of infrared radiation escaping from the atmosphere into space—an indirect measure of how much heat is being trapped. In the part of the infrared spectrum trapped by CO_2 —wavelengths between 13 and 19 micrometers—they found that between 1970 and 1997 less and less radiation was escaping. They concluded that the increasing quantity of atmospheric CO_2 was trapping energy that used to escape, and storing it in the atmosphere as heat. The results for the other greenhouse gases were similar.

These uncontested facts are enough to establish that "anthropogenic" greenhouse gas emissions are tending to make the atmosphere warmer. What's more, there is little doubt that the climate is changing right now. Temperature records from around the world going back 150 years suggest that 19 of the 20 warmest years—measured in terms of average global temperature, which takes account of all available thermometer data—have occurred since 1980, and that four of these occurred in the past seven years.

The only serious question mark over this record is the possibility that measurements have been biased by the growth of cities near the sites where temperatures are measured, as cities retain more heat than rural areas. But some new research suggests there is no such bias. David Parker of the UK's Met Office divided the historical temperature data into two sets: one taken in calm weather and the other in windy weather. He reasoned that any effect due to nearby cities would be more pronounced in calm conditions, when the wind could not disperse the heat. There was no difference.

It is at this point, however, that uncertainty starts to creep in. Take the grand claim made by some climate researchers that the 1990s were the warmest decade in the warmest century of the past millennium. This claim is embodied in the famous "hockey stick" curve, produced by Michael Mann of the University of Virginia in 1998, based on "proxy" records of past temperature, such as air bubbles in ice cores and growth rings in trees and coral. Sceptics have attacked the findings over poor methodology used, and their criticism has been confirmed by climate modellers, who have recently recognised that such proxy studies systematically underestimate past variability. As one Met Office scientist put it: "We cannot make claims as to the 1990s being the warmest decade."

There is also room for uncertainty in inferences drawn from the rise in temperature over the past 150 years. The warming itself is real enough, but that doesn't necessarily mean that human activity is to blame. Sceptics say that the warming could be natural, and again they have a point. It is now recognised that up to 40 per cent of the climactic variation since 1890 is probably due to two natural phenomena. The first is solar cycles, which influence the amount of radiation reaching the Earth, and some scientists have argued that increased solar activity can account for most of the warming of the past 150 years. The second is the changing frequency of volcanic eruptions, which produce airborne particles that can shade and hence cool the planet for a year or more. This does not mean, however, that the sceptics can claim victory, as no known natural effects can explain the 0.5 °C warming seen in the past 30 years. In fact, natural changes alone would have caused a marginal global cooling.

How Hot Will It Get?

In the face of such evidence, the vast majority of scientists, even sceptical ones, now agree that our activities are making the planet warmer, and that we can expect more warming as we release more CO_2 into the atmosphere. This leaves two critical questions. How much warming can we expect? And how much should we care about it? Here the uncertainties begin in earnest.

The concentration of CO_2 in the atmosphere now stands at around 375 parts per million. A doubling of CO_2 from pre-industrial levels of 280 parts per million, which could happen as early as 2050, will add only 1°C to average global temperatures, other things being equal. But if there's one thing we can count on, it is that other things will not be equal; some important things will change.

All experts agree that the planet is likely to respond in a variety of ways, some of which will dampen down the warming (negative feedback) while others will amplify it (positive feedback). Assessing the impacts of these feedbacks has been a central task of the UN's Intergovernmental Panel on Climate Change, a co-operative agency set up 17 years ago that has harnessed the work of thousands of scientists. Having spent countless hours of supercomputer time creating and refining models to stimulate the planet's climate system, the IPCC concludes that the feedbacks will be overwhelmingly positive. The only question, it says, is just how big this positive feedback will be.

The latest IPCC assessment is that doubling CO_2 levels will warm the world by anything from 1.4 to 5.8°C. In other words, this predicts a rise in global temperature from pre-industrial levels of around 14.8°C to between 16.2 and 20.6°C. Even at the low end, this is probably the biggest fluctuation in temperature that has occurred in the history of human civilisation. But uncertainties within the IPCC models remain, and the sceptics charge that they are so great that this conclusion is not worth the paper it is written on. So what are the positive feedbacks and how much uncertainty surrounds them?

Melting of polar ice is almost certainly one. Where the ice melts, the new, darker surface absorbs more heat from the sun, and so warms the planet. This is already happening. The second major source of positive feedback is water vapour. As this is responsible for a bigger slice of today's greenhouse effect than any other gas, including CO_2, any change in the amount of moisture in the atmosphere is critical. A warmer world will evaporate more water from the oceans, giving an extra push to warming. But there is a complication. Some of the water vapour will turn to cloud, and the net effect of cloudier skies and heat coming in and going out is far from clear. Clouds reflect energy from the sun back into space, but they also trap heat radiated from the surface, especially at night. Whether warming or cooling predominates depends on the type and height of clouds. The IPCC calculates that the combined effect of extra water vapour and clouds will increase warming, but accepts that clouds are the biggest source of uncertainty in the models.

Sceptics who pounce on such uncertainties should remember, however, that they cut both ways. Indeed, new research based on thousands of different climate simulation models run using the spare computing capacity of idling PCs, suggest that doubling CO_2 levels could increase temperatures by as much as 11°C. (*Nature*, vol. 434, p. 403)

Recent analysis suggests that clouds could have a more powerful warming effect than one thought—possibly much more powerful. (*New Scientist*, 24 July 2004, p. 44) And there could be other surprise positive feedbacks that do not yet feature in climate models. For instance, a release of some of the huge quantities of methane, a potent greenhouse gas, that are frozen into the Siberian permafrost and the ocean floor could have a catastrophic warming effect. And an end to ice formation in the Arctic could upset ocean currents even shut down the Gulf Stream—the starting point for the blockbuster movie *The Day After Tomorrow*.

There are counterbalancing negative feedbacks, some of which are already in the models. These include the ability of the oceans to absorb heat from the atmosphere, and of some pollutants—such as sulphate particles that make acid rain—to shade the planet. But both are double-edged. The models predict that the ocean's ability to absorb heat will decline as the surface warms, as mixing between less dense, warm surface waters and denser cold depths become more difficult. Meanwhile, sulphate and other aerosols could already be masking far stronger underlying warming effect than are apparent from measured temperatures. Aerosols last only a few weeks in the atmosphere, while greenhouse gases last for decades. So efforts to cut pollution by using technologies such as scrubbers to remove sulphur dioxide from power station stacks could trigger a surge in temperatures.

Sceptics also like to point out that most models do not yet include negative feedback from vegetation, which is already growing faster in a warmer world, and soaking up more CO_2. But here they may be onto a loser, as the few climate models so far include plants show that continued climate change is likely to damage their ability to absorb CO_2, potentially turning a negative feedback into a positive one.

Achilles' Heel?

More credible is the suggestion that some other important negative feedbacks have been left out. One prominent sceptic, meteorologist Richard Lindzen of the Massachusetts Institute of Technology, has made an interesting case that warming may dry out the upper levels of the innermost atmospheric layer, the troposphere, and less water means a weaker greenhouse effect.

Lindzen, who is one of the few sceptics with a research track record that most climate scientists respect, says this drying effect could negate all the positive feedbacks and bring the warming effect of a doubling of CO_2 levels back to 1°C. While there is little data to back up his idea, some studies suggest that these outer reaches are not as warm as IPCC models predict. This could be a mere wrinkle in the models or something more important. But if catastrophists have an Achilles' heel, this could be it.

Where does this leave us? Actually, with a surprising degree of consensus about the basic science of global warming—at least among scientists. As science historian Naomi Oreskes of the University of California, San Diego, wrote in *Science* late last year (vol. 306, p. 1686): "Politicians, economists, journalists and others have the impression of confusion, disagreement or discord among climate scientists, but that impression is incorrect."

Her review of all 928 peer-reviewed papers on climate change published between 1993 and 2003 showed the consensus to be real and near universal. Even sceptical scientists now accept that we can expect some warming. They differ from the rest only in that they believe most climate models overestimate the positive feedback and underestimate the negative, and they predict that warming will be at the bottom end of the IPCC's scale.

For the true hard-liners, of course, the scientific consensus must, by definition, be wrong. As far as they are concerned the thousands of scientists behind the IPCC models have either been seduced by their own doom-laden narrative or are engaged in a gigantic conspiracy. They say we are faced with what the philosopher of science Thomas Kuhn called a "paradigm problem."

"Most scientists spend their lives working to shore up the reigning world view—the dominant paradigm—and those who disagree are always much fewer in number," says climatologist Patrick Michaels of the University of Virginia in Charlottesville, a leading proponent of this view. The drive to conformity is accentuated by peer review, which ensures that only papers in support of the paradigm appear in the literature, Michaels says, and by public funding that gives money to research into the prevailing "paradigm of doom." Rebels who challenge prevailing orthodoxies are often proved right, he adds.

But even if you accept this sceptical view of how science is done, it doesn't mean the orthodoxy is always wrong. We know for sure that human activity is influencing the global environment, even if we don't know by how much. We might still get away with it: the sceptics could be right, and the majority of the world's climate scientists wrong. It would be a lucky break. But how lucky do you feel?

Meet the Sceptics

Most of the prominent organisations making the case against mainstream climate science have an avowed agenda of promoting free markets and minimal government. They often accept funding from the fossil-fuel industry. Few employ climate scientists.

1. **Competitive Enterprise Institute (Washington, DC).** A free-market lobby organisation that employs six experts on climate change. Two are lawyers, one an economist, one a political scientist, one a graduate in business studies and one a mathematician. They include economist Myron Ebell, most famous in the UK

for a tirade on BBC radio in November 2004 in which he accused the UK's government chief scientist David King of "knowing nothing about climate science." The institute receives funding from ExxonMobil, the world's largest oil company and an outspoken corporate opponent of mainstream climate science.

2. **American Enterprise Institute (Washington, DC).** Another free market think tank. The five experts it sent to the most recent negotiations on the Kyoto protocol, held in Buenos Aires, Argentina, in December, included just one natural scientist—a chemist. Receives money from ExxonMobil.

3. **George C. Marshall Institute (Washington, DC).** A think tank that has been promoting scepticism on climate change since 1989. It is a leading proponent of the argument that climate science is highly uncertain. Receives money from ExxonMobil.

4. **International Policy Network (London).** Free-market think tank which in November 2004 said global warming was a "myth," and described David King as "an embarrassment." Receives money from ExxonMobil.

5. **The scientists.** There are a few authoritative climate scientists in the sceptic camp. The most notable are Patrick Michaels from the University of Virginia, who is also the chief environmental commentator at the Cato Institute in Washington DC, and meteorologist Richard Lindzen from MIT. Most others are either retired, outside mainstream academia or tied to the fossil fuel industry. In the UK, three of the most prominent are Philip Stott, a retired biogeographer, former TV botanist David

Bellamy, and Martin Keeley, a palaeogeologist. Keeley argues on a BBC website that "global warming is a scam, perpetuated by scientists with vested interests." He is an oil exploration consultant.

Hotly Contested

1. Hockey stick hoo-ha

The term "hockey stick" was adopted by Michael Mann of the University of Virginia in 1998 to describe temperature changes over the past 1000 years, as identified from proxy data such as ice cores, tree rings and isotopic analysis of coral. This followed a largely flat line for 900 years (the stick's shaft), followed by soaring temperatures since 1900 (the blade). Sceptics say the methodology systematically underestimates past variability by smoothing out peaks and troughs, and they are winning the argument. Scientists at the UK Met Office and other IPCC stalwarts were among those who reported late last year in *Science* that the hockey stick analysis "contains assumptions that are not permissible." Nevertheless, even most sceptics accept direct measurements that show that the world has warmed in recent decades.

2. Sunspot squabble

While accepting that recent warming is real, some sceptics say solar cycles can explain most of the changes. This case was first made by Danish scientists Knud Lassen and Eigil Friis-Christensen in 1991. They found a correlation between sunspot activity and temperature changes on Earth from 1850 onwards. Time-based statistical correlations are notoriously tricky but it looked convincing, and prominent sceptics, including former

New Scientist editor Nigel Calder, took up the case. But more recent data has convinced Lassen that solar activity cannot explain the recent events. Sunspot activity since 1980 suggests that temperatures should have been stable or declining; in fact there has been a 0.4°C rise. That interpretation puts him in line with mainstream climate researchers.

3. Satellite data debacle

Sceptics have often claimed that satellite measurements show no appreciable trend in the temperature of much of the troposhere—the lowest layer of the atmosphere—since 1979. This has been interpreted variously as showing that warming is not extending into the atmosphere as far as models suggest it should, and that global warming itself is a myth. But much hangs on corrections that have to be made to the raw data to allow for cooling in the stratosphere—the next layer out—as a result of less heat radiating back from Earth. Two recent analyses of the satellite data suggest that the original interpretation was wrong, and that warming aloft has been in line with events on the ground. The jury is still out, but sceptics have largely dropped the case that the satellite data negates evidence of warming at Earth's surface.

Ross Gelbspan, a journalist with a long history of writing about climate change, took his peers to task in Mother Jones *for pandering to politicians and big businesses whose interests are in downplaying the impact of global warming.*

Gelbspan contends that journalistic coverage of this issue in print, electronic, and televised media is so limited in the United States in comparison to other nations that America's reporters should be ashamed. The results, he argues, have been tremendously effective. Although 90 percent of the world's scientists now agree that global warming is among the most significant problems facing our world, only a small margin of Americans—roughly 20 percent—fully understand the potential effects of global warming, the importance of creating policies to combat CO_2 emissions, or the need to support the research and development of renewable energy sources. —RC

"Snowed"
by Ross Gelbspan
Mother Jones, May/June 2005

When Southern California was inundated by a foot of rain, several feet of snow, and lethal mudslides earlier this year, the news reports made no mention of climate change—even though virtually all climate scientists agree that the first consequence of a warmer atmosphere is a marked increase in extreme weather events. When four hurricanes of extraordinary strength tore through Florida last fall, there was little media attention paid to the fact that hurricanes are made more intense by warming ocean surface waters. And when one storm dumped five feet of water on southern Haiti in 48 hours last spring, no coverage mentioned that an early manifestation of a warming atmosphere is a significant rise in severe downpours.

Though global climate change is breaking out all around us, the U.S. news media has remained silent. Not because climate change is a bad story—to the contrary: Conflict is the lifeblood of journalism, and the climate issue is riven with conflict. Global warming policy pits the United States against most of the countries of the world. It's a source of tension between the Bush administration and 29 states, nearly 100 cities, and scores of activist groups working to reduce emissions. And it has generated significant and acrimonious splits within the oil, auto, and insurance industries. These stories are begging to be written.

And they are being written—everywhere else in the world. One academic thesis completed in 2000 compared climate coverage in major U.S. and British newspapers and found that the issue received about three times as much play in the United Kingdom. Britain's *Guardian*, to pick an obviously liberal example, accorded three times more coverage to the climate story than the *Washington Post*, more than twice that of the *New York Times*, and nearly five times that of the *Los Angeles Times*. In this country, the only consistent reporting on this issue comes from the *New York Times'* Andrew C. Revkin, whose excellent stories are generally consigned to the paper's Science Times section, and the Weather Channel—which at the beginning of 2004 started including references to climate change in its projections, and even hired an on-air climate expert.

Why the lack of major media attention to one of the biggest stories of this century? The reasons have to do with the culture of newsrooms, the misguided application of journalistic balance, the very human tendency to deny the magnitude of so overwhelming a threat, and, last though not least, a decade-long campaign of deception, disinformation, and, at times, intimidation by the fossil fuel lobby to keep this issue off the public radar screen.

The carbon lobby's tactics can sometimes be heavy-handed; one television editor told me that his network had been threatened with a withdrawal of oil and automotive advertising after it ran a report suggesting a connection between a massive flood and climate change. But the most effective campaigns have been more subtly coercive. In the early 1990s, when climate scientists began to suspect that our burning of coal and oil was changing the earth's climate, Western Fuels, then a $400 million coal cooperative, declared in its annual report that it was enlisting several scientists who were skeptical about climate change—Patrick Michaels, Robert Balling, and S. Fred Singer—as spokesmen. The coal industry paid these and a handful of other skeptics some $1 million over a three-year period and sent them around the country to speak to the press and the public. According to internal strategy papers I obtained at the time, the purpose of the campaign was "to reposition global warming as theory (not fact)," with an emphasis on targeting "older, less educated males," and "younger, low-income women" in districts that received their electricity from coal, and who preferably had a representative on the House Energy and Commerce Committee.

The Western Fuels campaign was extraordinarily successful. In a *Newsweek* poll conducted in 1991, before the spin began, 35 percent of respondents said they "worry a great deal" about global warming. By 1997 that figure had dropped by one-third, to 22 percent.

Then as now, a prime tactic of the fossil fuel lobby centered on a clever manipulation of the ethic of journalistic balance. Any time reporters wrote stories about global warming, industry-funded naysayers demanded equal time in the name of balance. As a result, the press accorded the same weight to the industry-funded skeptics as it did to mainstream scientists, creating an enduring confusion in the public mind. To this day, many people are unsure whether global warming is real.

Journalistic balance comes into play when a story involves opinion: Should gay marriage be legal? Should we invade Iraq? Should we promote bilingual education or English immersion? For such stories an ethical journalist is obligated to give each competing view its most articulate presentation and roughly equivalent space.

But when the subject is a matter of fact, the concept of balance is irrelevant. What we know about the climate comes from the largest and most rigorously peer-reviewed scientific collaboration in history—the findings of more than 2,000 scientists from 100 countries reporting to the United Nations as the Intergovernmental Panel on Climate Change. The IPCC's conclusions, that the burning of fossil fuels is indeed causing significant shifts in the earth's climate, have been corroborated by the American Academy for the Advancement of Science, the American Geophysical Union, the American Meteorological Society, and the National Academy of Sciences. D. James Baker, former administrator of the National Oceanic and Atmospheric Administration, echoed many scientists when he said, "There is a better scientific consensus on this than on any other issue I know—except maybe Newton's second law of dynamics."

Granted, there are a few credentialed scientists who still claim climate change to be inconsequential. To give them their due, a reporter should learn where the weight of scientific opinion falls—and reflect that balance in his or her reporting. That would give mainstream scientists 95 percent of the story, with the skeptics getting a paragraph or two at the end.

But because most reporters don't have the time, curiosity, or professionalism to check out the science, they write equivocal stories with counter opposing quotes that play directly into the hands of the oil and coal industries by keeping the public confused.

Another major obstacle is the dominant culture of newsrooms. The fastest-rising journalists tend to make their bones covering politics, and so the lion's share of press coverage of climate change has focused on the political machinations surrounding global warming rather than its consequences. In 1997, when the Senate overwhelmingly passed a resolution against ratifying the Kyoto Protocol, the vote was covered as a political setback for the Clinton administration at the hands of congressional Republicans. (Predictably, the press paid little attention to a $13 million industry-funded advertising blitz in the run-up to that vote.) When President Bush pulled out of the Kyoto negotiating process in 2001, the coverage again focused not on the harm that would befall the planet as a result but on the resulting diplomatic tensions between the United States and the European Union.

Prior to 2001, Bush had declared he would not accept the findings of the IPCC—it was, after all, a U.N. body. "The jury's still out," he said, and called instead for a report from the National Academy of Sciences. That report, duly produced one month later, while professing uncertainty about exactly how much warming was attributable to one factor or another, affirmed that human activity was a major contributor. In covering Bush's call for an American climate report, few reporters bothered to check whether the academy had already taken a position; had they done so, they would have found that as early as 1992, it had recommended strong measures to minimize climate impacts.

Finally, coverage of the climate crisis is one of many casualties of media conglomeration. With most news outlets now owned by major corporations and faceless investors, marketing strategy is replacing news judgment; celebrity coverage is on the rise, even as newspapers cut staff and fail to provide their remaining reporters the time they need to research complex stories.

Ultimately, however, the responsibility for the failure of the press lies neither with the carbon lobby nor with newsroom culture or even the commercialization of the news. It lies in the indifference or laziness of hundreds of editors and thousands of reporters who are betraying their professional obligation to their readers and viewers. Climate change constitutes an immense drama of very uncertain outcome. It is as important and compelling a story as any reporter could hope to work on. Perversely, for so great an opportunity, it is threatening to become the shame of the American press.

In this report from the National Research Council, scientists argue the need for United States leaders to implement

a "no regrets" policy regarding the possibility that global warming could occur more rapidly than previously imagined. Basing their hypothesis on scientific findings, such as the information found in tree rings and ice cores, they found that abrupt climate changes (dramatic shifts in temperature that occur within a decade) have occurred several times over the past 100,000 years and are likely to occur again. And although the majority of scientists agree that there are many variables that will influence the rate of temperature change, they urge policy makers to improve our current understanding of global warming through the creation of better environmental models and improved education. Above all, the scientists responsible for this report noted that a proactive approach to determining the effects of global warming is needed to increase the resiliency of market and ecological systems. —RC

Abrupt Climate Change: Inevitable Surprises
by Richard B. Alley, Jochem Marotzke, William Nordhaus, Jonathan Overpeck, Dorothy Peteet, Roger Pielke Jr., Raymond Pierrehumbert, Peter Rhines, Thomas Stocker, Lynne Talley, and J. Michael Wallace
2002

Until the 1990s, the dominant view of climate change was that Earth's climate system has changed gradually in response to both natural and human-induced processes. Evidence pieced together over the last few decades, however, shows that climate has changed much more rapidly—sometimes abruptly—in the past and therefore could do so again in the future.

Abrupt climate change generally refers to a large shift in climate that persists for years of longer—such as marked changes in average temperature, or altered patterns of storms, floods, or droughts—over a widespread area such as an entire country or continent, that takes place so rapidly and unexpectedly that human or natural systems have difficulty adapting to it. In the context of past abrupt climate change, "rapidly" typically means on the order of a decade.

Severe droughts and other past abrupt climate changes have had demonstrable, adverse effects on human societies. While it is important not to be fatalistic about the threats posed by abrupt climate change, denying the likelihood or downplaying the relevance of past abrupt events could be costly. Increased knowledge is the best way to improve the effectiveness of response; research into the causes, patterns, and likelihood of abrupt climate change can help reduce vulnerabilities and increase our ability to adapt.

Evidence of Abrupt Climate Change

Researchers first became intrigued by abrupt climate change when they discovered striking evidence of large, abrupt, and widespread changes preserved in paleoclimatic archives—the history of Earth's climate recorded in tree rings, ice cores, sediments, and other sources. For example, tree rings show the frequency of droughts, sediments reveal the number and type of organisms present, and gas bubbles trapped in ice cores indicate past atmospheric conditions. With such techniques, researchers have discovered repeated instances of large and abrupt climate changes over the last 100,000 years during the slide into and the climb out of the most recent ice age—local warmings as great as 28 °F (–2°C) occurred repeatedly, sometimes in the mere span of a decade.

Some of the best known and most well studied widespread abrupt climate changes started and ended the Younger Dryas cold interval, a near global event that began abruptly about 12,800 years ago and ended even more suddenly about 11,600 years ago. Climate records show that much of the northern hemisphere was affected by extraordinary cold, dry, windy, conditions; dust and other wind-blown materials were more abundant in Greenland by a factor of 3 to 7, and methane concentrations were lower indicting a loss of wetland areas, among other evidence. The 110,000-year long ice-core records from central Greenland, and many other climate records, indicate that the Younger Dryas was one in a long string of abrupt climate changes.

More recently, less dramatic though still rapid climate changes have continued to occur. For example, a multidecadal drought is implicated in the collapse of the classic Mayan civilization in the ninth century. Paleoclimatic records from the last 10,000 years include apparent abrupt shifts in hurricane frequency, flood regimes, and droughts. Examples of abrupt changes in the past century alone include the rapid warming of the North Atlantic from 1920 to 1930 and the Dust Bowl drought of the 1930s.

Triggers of Abrupt Climate Change

Abrupt climate change can occur when the Earth's system get pushed across a threshold, whether by some sudden event like a massive volcanic eruption or by the accumulation of more gradual forces, or "forcings" on the system. Much as the slowly increasing pressure of a finger eventually flips a switch and abruptly turns on a light, or as a passenger's leaning more and more over the side of a canoe will at some point cause the craft to suddenly capsize, the slow effects of drifting continents or wobbling orbits or changing atmospheric composition may "switch" the climate to a new state. The more rapid the forcing, the more likely it is that it will "flip a switch," causing an abrupt change on the time scale of human economies or global ecosystems. Such forcings may occur through perturbations in key components of the Earth system such as:

> **Oceans.** Because water has enormous heat capacity, oceans typically store 10-100 times more heat than equivalent land surfaces. Thus the oceans exert a profound influence on climate through their ability to transport heat from one location to another. Changes in ocean circulation, and especially the thermohaline circulation in the North Atlantic have been implicated in abrupt climate change of the past such as the Younger Dryas. Floods of the glacial melt waters that would have freshened the North Atlantic and reduced the ability of its waters to sink, immediately preceded the cooling of the Younger Dryas and another short cold event 8,200 years ago, suggesting causation.

Cryosphere. The portion of the Earth covered in ice and snow, the cryosphere, greatly affects temperature. When sea ice forms, it increases the planetary reflective capacity, thereby enhancing cooling. Sea ice also insulates the atmosphere from the relatively warm ocean, allowing winter air temperatures to steeply decline and reduce the supply of moisture to the atmosphere. Glaciers and snow cover on land can also provide abrupt-change mechanisms. The water frozen in a glacier can melt if warmed sufficiently, leading to possibly rapid discharge, with consequent effects on sea level and atmospheric flow patterns. Meanwhile, snow-covered lands of all types maintain cold conditions because of their high reflectivity and because surface temperatures cannot rise above freezing until the snow melts.

Atmosphere. The atmosphere is involved in virtually every physical process of potential importance to abrupt climate change, providing a means of rapidly propagating the influence of any climate forcing from one part of the globe to another. Atmospheric temperature, composition, humidity, cloudiness, and wind determine the Earth's energy fluxes. Wind fields help dictate the ocean's surface circulation and upwelling patterns. Atmospheric-moisture transport—most prominently, through precipitation—helps govern the freshwater balance, overall water circulation, and the dynamics of glaciers.

Land surface. The reflective capacity of the land can change greatly, with fresh snow or ice sheets reflecting more than 90% of the sunlight striking them while dense forests absorb more than 90%. Changes in surface characteristics can also affect solar heating, cloud formation, rainfall, and surface-water flow to the oceans, thus feeding back strongly on climate.

External factors. Phenomena external to the climate system can also be agents of abrupt climate change. For example, the orbital parameters of the Earth vary over time, affecting the planet's distribution of solar energy. Fluctuations in solar output—prompted by sunspot activity or the effects of solar wind— may cause major climate fluctuations. The drying of the Sahara in the Holocene is linked to variations in the Earth's orbit around the sun.

Global Warming as a Possible Trigger

Greenhouse gases such as carbon dioxide are accumulating in the Earth's atmosphere and causing surface air temperatures and subsurface ocean temperatures to rise. These gradual changes, along with other human alterations of the climate system (e.g., land-use changes), are producing conditions in the Earth's climate that are outside the range of recent historical experience. Although it is not known whether these or future changes will trigger more abrupt climate changes, past abrupt climate changes have been especially common when the climate system itself was being altered.

A question of great societal relevance is whether the North Atlantic circulation, including the Gulf Stream, will remain stable under the global warming that is expected to continue for the next few centuries. A shutdown of the circulation would not induce a new ice age, but would cause major changes both in the ocean (major circulation regimes, upwelling and sinking regions, distribution of seasonal sea ice, ecological systems, and sea level) and in the atmosphere (land-sea temperature contrast, and the intensity, frequency, and paths of storms).

Other potential impacts of a global-warming induced abrupt climate change could be associated with increased frequency of extreme events related to land-surface hydrology. Great variability in precipitation patterns, ranging from heavy rainstorms and flooding to persistent drought, might become more common. In particular, some models suggest that greenhouse warming will cause El Niño manifestations to become stronger and more frequent. It is important to note that not all models agree on the potential impacts of global warming on abrupt climate change.

Improving Our Understanding

Scientists don't know enough about the details of abrupt climate change to accurately predict it. With better information, society could take more confident action to reduce the potential impact of abrupt changes on agriculture, water resources, and the built environment, among other impacts. A better understanding through research of such things as sea-ice and glacier stability, land-surface processes, and atmospheric and oceanic circulation patterns is needed. Moreover, to effectively use any additional knowledge of these and other physical processes behind abrupt climate change, more sophisticated ways of assessing their interactions must be developed including:

Better models. At present, the models used to assess climate and its impacts cannot simulate the size, speed, and extent of past abrupt changes, let alone predict future abrupt changes. Efforts are needed to improve how the mechanisms driving abrupt climate are represented in these models and to more rigorously test models against the climate record.

More paleoclimatic data. More climate information from the distant past would go a long way toward strengthening our understanding of abrupt climate changes and our models of past climate. In particular, and enhanced effort is needed to expand the geographic coverage, temporal resolution, and variety of paleoclimatic data.

Appropriate statistical tools. Because most statistical calculations at present are based on the assumption that climates are not changing but are stationary, they have limited value for nonstationary (changing) climates and for climate-related variables that are often highly skewed by rapid changes over time—such as for abrupt-change regimes. Available statistical tools themselves need to be adapted or replaced with new approaches altogether to better reflect the properties of abrupt climate change.

Ecological and Economic Impacts

One way of understanding the potential impacts of abrupt climate change is to think about how it could disrupt the timely replacement, repair, or adaptation of "capital stocks," whether of natural systems or nations' economies. For example, a rapid sea-level rise could inundate or threaten coastal populations; significant changes in patterns of droughts or frosts could destroy forests or agricultural systems; and sudden temperature shifts could render improperly insulated, heated, or cooled buildings uninhabitable.

To date, however, relatively little research has addressed the ecological and economic impacts of abrupt climate change; most studies focus on gradual climate change. Given the accumulating evidence of past abrupt changes and their capacity to affect human societies, some attention should be focused on potential future abrupt change scenarios. Concurrently, impact-assessment models need to be made increasingly sophisticated so they can accommodate diverse variables and represent interactions and outcomes in ways that more closely approximate reality.

Adapting to Abrupt Climate Change

Although our understanding of the causes and consequences of relatively abrupt changes in climate is imperfect, it makes sense to develop practical strategies that could be used to reduce economic and ecological systems' vulnerabilities to change. In that spirit, it is worth investigating "no-regrets" policies that provide benefits whether an abrupt climate change ultimately occurs or not. By moving scientific and public-policy research in directions that enhance system adaptability, it might be possible to reduce vulnerability at little or no net cost.

For example, the phase-out of chloro-fluorocarbons over the past two decades, and their replacement with relatively benign gases having shorter atmospheric residence times, reduced nations' contributions to global warming while also diminishing the risks posed by ozone depletion.

No-regrets measures in anticipation of abrupt climate change could include low-cost steps to: slow climate change; improve climate forecasting; slow biodiversity loss; improve water, land, and air quality; render institutions more robust to major disruptions; and adopt technological innovations that increase the resiliency of market and ecological systems.

The potential value of such measures is not restricted to the United States. With growing globalization, adverse social and economic impacts are now more likely than ever to spill across national boundaries. It is especially important that the needs of poorer countries, which could be highly vulnerable to the effects of abrupt climate change, be given sufficient attention and support.

Potential No-Regrets Strategies

The report highlights a few policy areas to explore in developing no-regrets options:

> **Energy policies.** Options to slow climate change, such as moving away from coal-burning toward other fuels, can also have benefits in reducing health or environmental effects of emissions.
>
> **Ecological policies.** In land-use and coastal planning, managers may be helped by information on the effects of nonlinear climate changes on ecosystems. Scientists and government

organizations at various levels could collaborate to develop and implement regulations and policies that reduce environmental degradation of water, air, and biota.

Forecasting of weather and weather-related events. The frequency and intensity of hurricanes and other storms could increase as a result of abrupt climate change, having large societal impacts. Efforts to improve forecasting and alert capabilities can reduce the loss of life by facilitating evacuations.

Institutions. Research should be conducted on improved institutions that will allow societies to withstand the greater risks associated with climate change, for example, water systems that better withstand drought, and insurance systems that hold up to increased demands to losses due to fire, floods, and storms.

Respected scientists throughout the world have long predicted that the pace of climate change in the Arctic might very well be greater, or at least more obvious, than the rate of change in more temperate regions. This speculation was recently confirmed in several reports published in 2004 and 2005, finding substantial evidence that the rate of warming in the northernmost regions is roughly ten times greater than that of the rest of the world. One factor that scientists

*believe might be influencing this trend is albedo, or the
heat-reflecting value of ice. When glacier ice melts, it can
no longer reflect the sun's rays. As rock layers once hidden
beneath the ice are exposed, the sections of exposed earth
absorb heat, accelerating the melting process.*

*Unfortunately, as the environmental stability changes in the
region, so must the lifestyles of the people and the animals
that call the Arctic their home. In this* New York Times
*article, writer Andrew C. Revkin draws much-needed atten-
tion to the human side of global warming by considering
the effect of these environmental changes on the Inuit population of the Arctic. —RC*

"Eskimos Seek to Recast Global Warming as a Rights Issue"
by Andrew C. Revkin
New York Times, December 15, 2004

The Eskimos, or Inuit, about 155,000 seal-hunting peoples
scattered around the Arctic, plan to seek a ruling from the
Inter-American Commission on Human Rights that the United
States, by contributing substantially to global warming, is
threatening their existence.

The Inuit plan is part of a broader shift in the debate
over human-caused climate change evident among participants
in the 10th round of international talks taking place in Buenos
Aires aimed at averting dangerous human interference with
the climate system.

Inuit leaders said they planned to announce the effort at
the climate meeting today.

Representatives of poor countries and communities—from the Arctic fringes to the atolls of the tropics to the flanks of the Himalayas—say they are imperiled by rising temperatures and seas through no fault of their own. They are casting the issue as no longer simply an environmental problem but as an assault on their basic human rights.

The commission, an investigative arm of the Organization of American States, has no enforcement powers. But a declaration that the United States has violated the Inuit's rights could create the foundation for an eventual lawsuit, either against the United States in an international court or against American companies in federal court, said a number of legal experts, including some aligned with industry.

Such a petition could have decent prospects now that industrial countries, including the United States, have concluded in recent reports and studies that warming linked to heat-trapping smokestack and tailpipe emissions is contributing to big environmental changes in the Arctic, a number of experts said.

Last month, an assessment of Arctic climate change by 300 scientists for the eight countries with Arctic territory, including the United States, concluded that "human influences" are now the dominant factor.

Inuit representatives attending the conference said in telephone interviews that after studying the matter for several years with the help of environmental lawyers they would this spring begin the lengthy process of filing a petition by collecting videotaped statements from elders and hunters about the effects they were experiencing from the shrinking northern icescape.

The lawyers, at EarthJustice, a nonprofit San Francisco law firm, and the Center for International Environmental

Law, in Washington, said the Inter-American Commission, which has a record of treating environmental degradation as a human rights matter, provides the best chance of success. The Inuit have standing in the Organization of American States through Canada.

Sheila Watt-Cloutier, the elected chairwoman of the Inuit Circumpolar Conference, the quasi-governmental group recognized by the United Nations as representing the Inuit, said the biggest fear was not that warming would kill individuals but that it would be the final blow to a sturdy but suffering culture.

"We've had to struggle as a people to keep afloat, to keep our indigenous wisdom and traditions," she said. "We're an adaptable people, but adaptability has its limits."

"Something is bound to give, and it's starting to give in the Arctic, and we're giving that early warning signal to the rest of the world."

If the Inuit effort succeeds, it could lead to an eventual stream of litigation, somewhat akin to lawsuits against tobacco companies, legal experts said.

The two-week convention, which ends Friday, is the latest session on two climate treaties: the 1992 framework convention on climate change and the Kyoto Protocol, an addendum that takes effect in February [2005] and for the first time requires most industrialized countries to curb such emissions.

The United States has signed both pacts and is bound by the 1992 treaty, which requires no emissions cuts. But the Bush administration opposes the mandatory Kyoto treaty, saying it could harm the economy and unfairly excuses big developing countries from obligations.

That situation makes the United States particularly vulnerable to such suits, environmental lawyers said.

By embracing the first treaty and signing the second, it has acknowledged that climate change is a problem to be avoided; but by subsequently rejecting the Kyoto pact, the lawyers said, it has not shown a commitment to stemming its emissions, which constitute a fourth of the global total.

The American delegation at the Buenos Aires conference declined to comment on Tuesday on the petition or the arguments behind it. "Until the Inuit have presented a complaint, we are not responding to that issue," a State Department official said. "When they do, we will look at what they have to say, consider it and then respond."

Christopher C. Horner, a lawyer for the Cooler Heads Coalition, an industry-financed group opposed to cutting the emissions, said the chances of success of such lawsuits had risen lately.

From his standpoint, he said, "The planets are aligned very poorly."

Delegates who flew to the conference from the Arctic's far-flung communities, where retreating sea ice imperils traditional seal hunts, said they planned to meet in Buenos Aires with representatives from small-island nations that could eventually be swamped by rising seas, swelled by meltwater from shrinking glaciers and Arctic ice sheets.

Enele S. Sopoaga, the ambassador to the United Nations from Tuvalu, a 15-foot-high nation of wave-pounded atolls halfway between Australia and Hawaii, said he still saw legal efforts as a last resort.

Tuvalu had threatened to sue the United States two years ago in the International Court of Justice, but held off for a variety of reasons.

CHAPTER FIVE

POWER, AUTHORITY, AND GOVERNANCE: WHAT IS THE GOVERNMENT'S ROLE IN THE PREVENTION OF CLIMATE CHANGE?

As the human contribution to the increase in greenhouse gases is acknowledged—even among skeptics—the debate surrounding global warming will change. Rather than questioning whether humans contribute to global warming, people will ask what the government's role is in protecting the environment. Although the long-awaited Kyoto Protocol was signed by 141 nations on February 16, 2005, the United States opted out of the agreement, voicing its concerns about adverse effects on the U.S. economy. Still, proponents of the Kyoto Protocol insist that the agreement is only a foundation for future emissions reductions. (Even if the agreement is completely successful, it is only expected to reduce global temperatures by between 32.04°F (0.02°C) and 32.05°F (0.28°C) by 2050— a minuscule decrease when compared to the rate at which they are currently rising.) The following article discusses what role government should take in trying to control carbon emissions and also raises concerns about methane gases, which some estimate may speed the warming process more rapidly than carbon gases do. —RC

From "Global Warming and Its Dangers"
by J. R. Clark and Dwight R. Lee
Independent Review, Spring 2004

We admit at the outset that we know little about the science of global warming. How much, if at all, the earth is warming; whether any warming is a trend or the result of random variations in global weather patterns; and, if a warming trend does exist, how much of it is owing to human activity are questions we cannot answer. Perhaps this ignorance protects us against anxiety attacks when we hear frightening accounts of what lies in store for the planet earth and its inhabitants if governments do not immediately take bold and decisive control of the global climate. Our serenity, however, more likely arises from our exposure to public-choice analysis, which convinced us that concern about global warming is being inflamed and inflated as an open-ended rationale for expanding government control over the economy even further. This conviction does not leave us entirely sanguine, however, because we believe a serious danger of this rush to regulate is going largely unnoticed—a danger that might make any actual global warming a far greater problem than it should be.

First, the Bad News

People are easily frightened, and when they are, governments grow. Fear and crises go hand in hand, and the evidence that government thrives in crises, real or imagined, is overwhelming (Higgs 1987). Claims of impending environmental crisis have proved especially effective in helping to justify an expanded role for government over the past thirty-five years.

Widespread famine, acid rain, resource depletion, global cooling (yes, that's right—a big concern in the 1970s), lack of landfills, Alar-laced apples, the spotted owl's possible extinction, and urban sprawl are but a few of the alleged crises used in recent years to justify more reliance on government coercion and less reliance on market incentives . . .

Not surprisingly, the latest episode in this escalating series of crises, global warming, is being described in apocalyptic terms. For example, in *World on Fire: Saving an Endangered Earth*, former Senate leader George Mitchell informs us that global warming, if left unchecked, "would trigger meteorological chaos—raging hurricanes...capable of killing millions of people; . . . record-breaking heat waves; and profound drought that could drive Africa and the entire Indian subcontinent over the edge into mass starvation . . . Unchecked, [global warming] would match nuclear war in its potential for devastation" (qtd. in Moore 1995, 83).[1] If this dire prediction is not frightening enough for you, search the combination of key words global warming and catastrophic on Google.com, and you will find comments that make Mitchell's account appear sanguine.

We do not want to leave the impression that the global-warming hawks bear only bad news. They invariably soften the threat of doom with the good news that because global warming results from human activity (they ignore what seems to be a warming trend on Mars), we can reserve its destructive effects by changing our behavior. Furthermore, we fortunately have "experts" who know what changes should be made, so our salvation requires only that we give these experts the necessary power and money. This reassuring news does raise a slight problem, however: the experts recommend changes that require government either directly or indirectly to impose controls over almost every aspect of our lives. Greenhouse gas emissions, understood as causes of global warming, now are being defined as pollutants that must be reduced significantly below current levels (as required, at least for developed nations, by the Kyoto Protocol). Carbon dioxide is receiving the most attention, and reducing it as recommended would require lifestyle changes in the developed world, affecting everything from the types of products we consume to the type of occupations we pursue, and would almost surely force the less developed world to stay that way.[2] The cost of reducing carbon dioxide can be minimized (though remaining huge) by creating global markets for permits to emit carbon dioxide, but the parties whose interests are attached to government control strenuously oppose such markets. Yet even if these markets were created, they would be distorted significantly by direct government controls and by politically influential groups more interested in protecting their interests than in protecting the environment. Absent markets, political attempts to prevent global warming will result in the substitution of government regulations for both private property and market exchange on an enormous scale.

The Best Solution: Freedom and Prosperity

We admit that without government action, market incentives probably will not reduce greenhouse gas emissions in the short run. However, government regulations that undermine both information flows and adjustments of the market process in an effort to reduce greenhouse gases, even if successful, run the serious risk of increasing the long-run damage of any global warming that does occur.

Two possible, and opposing, approaches to global warming present themselves. The first, and the most familiar one, is the use of government regulations to force greenhouse gas reductions. The second approach is to emphasize arrangements that allow the most efficient response to any changes in the global climate that do occur, without trying to prevent such changes. The latter approach avoids government actions that interfere with the superior ability of markets to provide the information and motivation necessary to adapt quickly and approximately to changing conditions. Although this approach may not do as much as direct government action to reduce global warming, it results in better responses to any given increase (or decease) in global temperatures. So, even if warming is greater under the market approach that it is under the government approach, the former may still be preferable. A more efficient response to a worse situation can be better than a less efficient response to a better situation.

Even if the government approach is better than the market approach in reducing greenhouse gases, this success may have little, if any, effect on global temperatures, given the rather minor proportion to total carbon dioxide emissions from human activities.[3] Furthermore, over the long run, the innovation fostered by the disciplined freedom of the market may offer the best hope for reducing reliance on the fossil fuels responsible for most human release of greenhouse gases.

Source Notes

1. Moore points out that the Earth has experienced times, including some in the past few hundred years, when the weather was substantially warmer that it is currently and that those times have been associated with bursts of human progress and improvements in living standards, whereas periods of cooler weather have been periods of stagnation and worse (1995,83).

2. The human role in carbon dioxide discharges is modest compared to nature's. According to Easterbrook, "naturally occurring carbon emissions outnumber human-caused emissions roughly 29 to one" (1995, 312). Interestingly, some scientists believe that methane may contribute as much to global warming as carbon dioxide does, because, though less prevalent, it is far more effective in trapping heat. Moreover, methane reduction would be much less costly. See Easterbrook (1995, 298–300) for the advantages of focusing on methane and for some of the special-interest opposition to doing so.

3. This argument is stronger for carbon dioxide than for methane emissions, which, as noted previously, are more easily reduced and may be as responsible for global warming.

In this article, Fortune *writer David Stipp interprets a report released in 2004 by the Pentagon about the possibility of a dramatic and fast-paced change in climate that could send the United States and Europe into another ice age. Although news of the report made headlines around the world, its authors, Peter Schwartz and Doug Randall, two Bay Area futurologists, later commented that the report was "improbable and extremely unlikely." The Department of Defense's Andrew Marshall, the man who commissioned the report, later issued a statement to put it in context. According to a February 25, 2004, edition of the* San Francisco Chronicle, *Marshall said, "The Schwartz and Randall study reflects the limits of scientific models and information when it comes to predicting the effects of abrupt global warming. Although there is significant scientific evidence on this issue, much of what this study predicts is still speculation." —RC*

"The Pentagon's Weather Nightmare"
by David Stipp
Fortune, **February 9, 2004**

Global warming may be bad news for future generations, but let's face it, most of us spend as little time worrying about it as we did about al-Qaeda before 9/11. Like the terrorists, though, the seemingly remote climate risk may hit home sooner and harder than we ever imagined. In fact, the prospect has become so real that the Pentagon's strategic planners are grappling with it.

The threat that has riveted their attention is this: Global warming, rather than causing gradual, centuries-spanning change, may be pushing the climate to a tipping point. Growing evidence suggests the ocean-atmosphere system that controls the world's climate can lurch from one state to another in less than a decade—like a canoe that's gradually tilted until suddenly it flips over. Scientists don't know how close the system is to a critical threshold. But abrupt climate change may well occur in the not-too-distant future. If it does, the need to rapidly adapt may overwhelm many societies—thereby upsetting the geopolitical balance of power.

Though triggered by warming, such change would probably cause cooling in the Northern Hemisphere, leading to longer, harsher winters in much of the U.S. and Europe. Worse, it would cause massive droughts, turning farmland to dust bowls and forests to ashes. Picture last fall's California wildfires as a regular thing. Or imagine similar disasters destabilizing nuclear powers such as Pakistan or Russia—it's easy to see why the Pentagon has become interested in abrupt climate change.

Climate researchers began getting seriously concerned about it a decade ago, after studying temperature indicators embedded in ancient layers of Arctic ice. The data show that a number of dramatic shifts in average temperature took place in the past with shocking speed—in some cases, just a few years.

The case for angst was buttressed by a theory regarded as the most likely explanation for the abrupt changes. The eastern U.S. and northern Europe, it seems, are warmed by a huge Atlantic Ocean current that flows north from the tropics—that's why Britain, at Labrador's latitude, is relatively temperate. Pumping out warm, moist air, this "great conveyor" current gets cooler and denser as it moves north. That causes the current to sink in the North Atlantic, where it heads south again in the ocean depths. The sinking process draws more water from the south, keeping the roughly circular current on the go.

But when the climate warms, according to the theory, fresh water from melting Arctic glaciers flows into the North Atlantic, lowering the current's salinity—and its density and tendency to sink. A warmer climate also increases rainfall and runoff into the current, further lowering its saltiness. As a result, the conveyor loses its main motive force and can rapidly collapse, turning off the huge heat pump and altering the climate over much of the Northern Hemisphere.

Scientists aren't sure what caused the warming that triggered such collapses in the remote past. (Clearly it wasn't humans and their factories.) But the data from Arctic ice and other sources suggest the atmospheric changes that preceded earlier collapses were dismayingly similar to today's global warming. As the Ice Age began drawing to a close about 13,000 years ago, for example, temperatures in Greenland rose to levels near those of recent decades. Then they abruptly plunged as the conveyor apparently shut down, ushering in the "Younger Dryas" period, a 1,300-year reversion to ice-age conditions. (A dryas is an Arctic flower that flourished in Europe at the time.)

Though Mother Nature caused past abrupt climate changes, the one that may be shaping up today probably has more to do with us. In 2001 an international panel of climate experts concluded that there is increasingly strong evidence that most of the global warming observed over the past 50 years is attributable to human activities—mainly the burning of fossil fuels such as oil and coal, which release heat-trapping carbon dioxide. Indicators of the warming include shrinking Arctic ice, melting alpine glaciers, and markedly earlier springs at northerly latitudes. A few years ago such changes seemed signs of possible trouble for our kids or grandkids. Today they seem portents of a cataclysm that may not conveniently wait until we're history.

Accordingly, the spotlight in climate research is shifting from gradual to rapid change. In 2002 the National Academy of Sciences issued a report concluding that human activities could trigger abrupt change. Last year the World Economic Forum in Davos, Switzerland, included a session at which Robert Gagosian, director of the Woods Hole Oceanographic Institution in Massachusetts, urged policymakers to consider the implications of possible abrupt climate change within two decades.

Such jeremiads are beginning to reverberate more widely. Billionaire Gary Comer, founder of Lands' End, has adopted abrupt climate change as a philanthropic cause. Hollywood has also discovered the issue—next summer 20th Century Fox is expected to release *The Day After Tomorrow*, a big-budget disaster movie starring Dennis Quaid as a scientist trying to save the world from an ice age precipitated by global warming.

Fox's flick will doubtless be apocalyptically edifying. But what would abrupt climate change really be like?

Scientists generally refuse to say much about that, citing a data deficit. But recently, renowned Department of Defense planner Andrew Marshall sponsored a groundbreaking effort to come to grips with the question. A Pentagon legend, Marshall, 82, is known as the Defense Department's "Yoda"—a balding, bespectacled sage whose pronouncements on looming risks have long had an outsized influence on defense policy. Since 1973 he has headed a secretive think tank whose role is to envision future threats to national security. The Department of Defense's push on ballistic-missile defense is known as his brainchild. Three years ago Defense Secretary Donald Rumsfeld picked him to lead a sweeping review on military "transformation," the shift toward nimble forces and smart weapons.

When scientists' work on abrupt climate change popped onto his radar screen, Marshall tapped another eminent visionary, Peter Schwartz, to write a report on the national-security implications of the threat. Schwartz formerly headed planning at Royal Dutch/Shell Group and has since consulted with organizations ranging from the CIA to DreamWorks—he helped create futuristic scenarios for Steven Spielberg's film *Minority Report*. Schwartz and co-author Doug Randall at the Monitor Group's Global Business Network, a scenario-planning think tank in Emeryville, Calif., contacted top climate experts and pushed them to talk about what-ifs that they usually shy away from—at least in public.

The result is an unclassified report, completed late last year, that the Pentagon has agreed to share with *Fortune*. It doesn't pretend to be a forecast. Rather, it sketches a dramatic but plausible scenario to help planners think about coping strategies. Here is an abridged version:

A total shutdown of the ocean conveyor might lead to a big chill like the Younger Dryas, when icebergs appeared as far south as the coast of Portugal. Or the conveyor might only temporarily slow down, potentially causing an era like the "Little Ice Age," a time of hard winters, violent storms, and droughts between 1300 and 1850. That period's weather extremes caused horrific famines, but it was mild compared with the Younger Dryas.

For planning purposes, it makes sense to focus on a midrange case of abrupt change. A century of cold, dry, windy weather across the Northern Hemisphere that suddenly came on 8,200 years ago fits the bill—its severity fell between that of the Younger Dryas and the Little Ice Age. The event is thought to have been triggered by a conveyor collapse after a time of rising temperatures not unlike today's global warming. Suppose it recurred, beginning in 2010. Here are some of the things that might happen by 2020:

At first the changes are easily mistaken for normal weather variation—allowing skeptics to dismiss them as a "blip" of little importance and leaving policymakers and the public paralyzed with uncertainty. But by 2020 there is little doubt that something drastic is happening. The average temperature has fallen by up to five degrees Fahrenheit in some regions of North America and Asia and up to six degrees in parts of Europe. (By comparison, the average temperature over the North Atlantic during the last ice age was ten to 15 degrees lower than it is today.) Massive droughts have begun in key agricultural regions. The average annual rainfall has dropped by nearly 30% in northern Europe, and its climate has become more like Siberia's.

Violent storms are increasingly common as the conveyor becomes wobbly on its way to collapse. A particularly severe storm causes the ocean to break through levees in the Netherlands, making coastal cities such as the Hague unlivable. In California the delta island levees in the Sacramento River area are breached, disrupting the aqueduct system transporting water from north to south.

Megadroughts afflict the U.S., especially in the southern states, along with winds that are 15% stronger on average than they are now, causing widespread dust storms and soil loss. The U.S. is better positioned to cope than most nations, however, thanks to its diverse growing climates, wealth, technology, and abundant resources. That has a downside, though: It magnifies the haves-vs.-have-nots gap and fosters bellicose finger-pointing at America.

Turning inward, the U.S. effectively seeks to build a fortress around itself to preserve resources. Borders are strengthened to hold back starving immigrants from Mexico, South America, and the Caribbean islands—waves of boat people pose especially grim problems. Tension between the U.S. and Mexico rises as the U.S. reneges on a 1944 treaty that guarantees water flow from the Colorado River into Mexico. America is forced to meet its rising energy demand with options that are costly both economically and politically, including nuclear power and onerous Middle Eastern contracts. Yet it survives without catastrophic losses.

Europe, hardest hit by its temperature drop, struggles to deal with immigrants from Scandinavia seeking warmer climes to the south. Southern Europe is beleaguered by refugees from hard-hit countries in Africa and elsewhere. But Western Europe's wealth helps buffer it from catastrophe.

Australia's size and resources help it cope, as does its location—the conveyor shutdown mainly affects the Northern Hemisphere. Japan has fewer resources but is able to draw on its social cohesion to cope—its government is able to induce population-wide behavior changes to conserve resources.

China's huge population and food demand make it particularly vulnerable. It is hit by increasingly unpredictable monsoon rains, which cause devastating floods in drought-denuded areas. Other parts of Asia and East Africa are similarly stressed. Much of Bangladesh becomes nearly uninhabitable because of a rising sea level, which contaminates inland water supplies. Countries whose diversity already produces conflict, such as India and Indonesia, are hard-pressed to maintain internal order while coping with the unfolding changes.

As the decade progresses, pressures to act become irresistible—history shows that whenever humans have faced a choice between starving or raiding, they raid. Imagine Eastern European countries, struggling to feed their populations, invading Russia—which is weakened by a population that is already in decline—for access to its minerals and energy supplies. Or picture Japan eyeing nearby Russian oil and gas reserves to power desalination plants and energy-intensive farming. Envision nuclear-armed Pakistan, India, and China skirmishing at their borders over refugees, access to shared rivers, and arable land. Or Spain and Portugal fighting over fishing rights—fisheries are disrupted around the world as water temperatures change, causing fish to migrate to new habitats.

Growing tensions engender novel alliances. Canada joins fortress America in a North American bloc. (Alternatively, Canada may seek to keep its abundant hydropower for itself,

straining its ties with the energy-hungry U.S.) North and
South Korea align to create a technically savvy, nuclear-armed
entity. Europe forms a truly unified bloc to curb its immigra-
tion problems and protect against aggressors. Russia,
threatened by impoverished neighbors in dire straits, may join
the European bloc.

Nuclear arms proliferation is inevitable. Oil supplies are
stretched thin as climate cooling drives up demand. Many
countries seek to shore up their energy supplies with nuclear
energy, accelerating nuclear proliferation. Japan, South Korea,
and Germany develop nuclear-weapons capabilities, as do Iran,
Egypt, and North Korea. Israel, China, India, and Pakistan
also are poised to use the bomb.

The changes relentlessly hammer the world's "carrying
capacity"—the natural resources, social organizations, and
economic networks that support the population. Technological
progress and market forces, which have long helped boost
Earth's carrying capacity, can do little to offset the crisis—it is
too widespread and unfolds too fast.

As the planet's carrying capacity shrinks, an ancient pattern reemerges: the eruption of desperate, all-out wars over
food, water, and energy supplies. As Harvard archeologist
Steven LeBlanc has noted, wars over resources were the norm
until about three centuries ago. When such conflicts broke out,
25% of a population's adult males usually died. As abrupt climate change hits home, warfare may again come to define
human life.

Over the past decade, data have accumulated suggesting
that the plausibility of abrupt climate change is higher than
most of the scientific community, and perhaps all of the political

community, are prepared to accept. In light of such findings, we should be asking when abrupt change will happen, what the impacts will be, and how we can prepare—not whether it will really happen. In fact, the climate record suggests that abrupt change is inevitable at some point, regardless of human activity. Among other things, we should:

- Speed research on the forces that can trigger abrupt climate change, how it unfolds, and how we'll know it's occurring.
- Sponsor studies on the scenarios that might play out, including ecological, social, economic, and political fallout on key food-producing regions.
- Identify "no regrets" strategies to ensure reliable access to food and water and to ensure our national security.
- Form teams to prepare responses to possible massive migration, and food and water shortages.
- Explore ways to offset abrupt cooling—today it appears easier to warm than to cool the climate via human activities, so there may be "geo-engineering" options available to prevent a catastrophic temperature drop.

In sum, the risk of abrupt climate change remains uncertain, and it is quite possibly small. But given its dire consequences, it should be elevated beyond a scientific debate. Action now matters, because we may be able to reduce its likelihood of happening, and we can certainly be better prepared if it does. It is time to recognize it as a national security concern.

The Pentagon's reaction to this sobering report isn't known—in keeping with his reputation for reticence, Andy Marshall declined to be interviewed. But the fact that he's concerned may signal a sea change in the debate about global warming. At least some federal thought leaders may be starting to perceive climate change less as a political annoyance and more as an issue demanding action.

If so, the case for acting now to address climate change, long a hard sell in Washington, may be gaining influential support, if only behind the scenes. Policymakers may even be emboldened to take steps such as tightening fuel-economy standards for new passenger vehicles, a measure that would simultaneously lower emissions of greenhouse gases, reduce America's perilous reliance on OPEC oil, cut its trade deficit, and put money in consumers' pockets. Oh, yes—and give the Pentagon's fretful Yoda a little less to worry about.

Rather than mourn the lack of involvement by some nations, specifically the United States, in addressing the obvious need to reduce carbon emissions around the world (carbon emissions have risen to 375 parts per billion in the past fifty years according to the IPCC), John Browne, head of British Petroleum (BP), urges the private sector to actively support a reduction in the release of greenhouse gases. In doing so, he continues, companies can increase

fossil fuel efficiency and help support the research and development of alternative, clean-burning energy sources. However, Browne urges government involvement in supporting education and research. Most of all, tax incentives for businesses would give them the economic jumpstart they need to make the dramatic changes necessary to improve our global environment. —RC

From "Beyond Kyoto"
by John Browne
Foreign Affairs, July/August 2004

In 1997, more than 180 countries gathered in Kyoto, Japan, in search of a coordinated international response to global warming. The provisional agreement they reached appeared to mark a significant step forward. But the Kyoto Protocol is coming unraveled. Despite nearly a decade of effort, it may not even enter into force as a binding instrument. Canada, Japan, and the European Union—the most enthusiastic advocates of the Kyoto process—are not on track to meet their commitments. And the United States has withdrawn from the agreement entirely. Those concerned with the sustainability of the earth's climate could be forgiven for feeling depressed.

Clear-eyed realism is essential. But dismay, however understandable, is a mistaken reaction. There is scope for a different and more positive view of the last seven years and of the future. First, it has become obvious that Kyoto was simply the starting point of a very long endeavor—comparable, perhaps, to the meetings in 1946 at which a group of 23 countries agreed to reduce tariffs. Those meetings set in

motion a process that led to the establishment of the
General Agreement on Tariffs and Trade in 1948, which, in
turn, led to the creation of the World Trade Organization in
the mid-1990s. Second, we have improved, if still imperfect,
knowledge of the challenges and uncertainties that climate
change presents, as well as a better understanding of the
time scales involved. Third, many countries and companies
have had experience reducing emissions and have proved
that such reductions can be achieved without destroying
competitiveness or jobs. Fourth, science and technology
have advanced on multiple fronts. And finally, public awareness of the issue has grown—not just in the developed
world but all around the globe . . .

Knowns and Unknowns

Before considering new approaches, it is necessary to distill
some basic facts from the voluminous, complex, and incomplete
scientific work on global warming.

Global temperatures have risen by about 0.6 degrees
Celsius since the nineteenth century. Other measures of climate bolster the theory that the world is getting warmer:
satellite measurements suggest that spring arrives about a
week earlier now than in the late 1970s, for example, and
records show that migratory birds fly to higher latitudes earlier in the season and stay later. According to the UN'S
Intergovernmental Panel on Climate Change (IPCC)—by far
the most authoritative body of scientists working on this
issue—humans are probably not responsible for all the measured warming. But the trend is undoubtedly due in large part
to substantial increases in carbon dioxide emissions from

human activity. Since the middle of the nineteenth century, the average concentration of carbon dioxide—a so-called greenhouse gas—in the world's atmosphere has risen from some 280 parts per million (ppm) to around 370 ppm. Burning fossil fuels account for about three-quarters of human emissions, with deforestation and changes in land use (mainly in the tropics) accounting for the rest.

There are two main reasons why it has been hard for societies to tackle climate change. First, carbon dioxide has a very long life span: it exists for hundreds of years in the atmosphere, making this a multigenerational issue. Second, reducing carbon dioxide in the atmosphere can be done only on a truly global basis, since emissions mix throughout the atmosphere much quicker than individual processes can limit their impact.

Beyond these known facts, the picture becomes murkier. For instance, nobody knows how rapidly emissions of carbon dioxide and other greenhouse gases will rise in the future. That outcome depends on the pace of global economic growth and on the impact of technology on the ways society generates and deploys useful energy. Equally, it is impossible to determine precisely how the climate will respond as greenhouse gases accumulate to ever-higher concentrations in the atmosphere. The brightness and altitude of clouds, for example, determine whether warming is amplified or diminished, yet it is not known how exactly climate change will affect cloud patterns. Nor is it known how the world's carbon cycle will respond. A warmer climate might make the planet greener—which would mean more carbon dioxide would be sucked from the atmosphere. Alternatively, climate change might impose such severe stress on the biosphere that nature's processes for removing carbon dioxide from the atmosphere would become less efficient than normal.

The most recent IPCC assessment, published in 2001, concludes that if no precautionary action is taken, carbon dioxide concentrations will rise by 2050 to between 450 and 550 ppm and will continue to increase throughout the twenty-first century. The IPCC estimates that temperatures will rise by between 0.5 degrees Celsius and 2.5 degrees Celsius by 2050, with an increase of 1.4 degrees to 5.8 degrees possible by 2100.

One of the most likely effects of global warming is a rise in sea level, as glaciers melt and warmer water expands in the oceans. The best projections suggest seas of between 5 centimeters and 32 centimeters higher by 2050; the outer limit projected for 2100 approaches one meter. These numbers seem small, but coastlines are shallow slopes, not firm walls, so a rise in water levels of just tens of centimeters would erase kilometers of wetlands and beaches.

Industrialized countries will probably be able to handle rising water levels, at least in the next few decades. London and cities in the Netherlands, for example, already have defenses to hold back surging seas. And farmers in wealthy countries can respond to changes in climate by adjusting irrigation and varying the crops they plant, in many cases with government financial support. But the developing world, home to four-fifths of humanity, is likely to fare considerably worse on both fronts. Hundreds of thousands of people have already been displaced by periodic flooding in Bangladesh, and subsistence farmers—who are far less adaptive than their richer counterparts—are already struggling at the Climactic margin.

The most dramatic scenarios, although unlikely, would have grave consequences for humanity and ecosystems. Rapid changes in climate could upset the circulation of the North Atlantic, for example—which, ironically, would cause much colder regional temperatures in northern Europe by weakening the heat-rich Gulf Stream. The Amazon rain forest could deplete dramatically due to drying in the atmosphere, in turn releasing huge volumes of carbon that is stored in trees. And an accelerated rise in sea level from melting ice in Antarctica could occur. These uncertain consequences do not lead to crisp timetables for policy. But they mean that precaution and improvements in measurement and learning will be crucial.

A sober strategy would ensure that any increase in the world's temperature is limited to between 2 or 3 degrees Celsius above the current level in the long run. Focused on that goal, a growing number of governments and experts have concluded that policy should aim to stabilize concentrations of carbon dioxide in the atmosphere in the range from 500 to 550 ppm over the next century, which is less than twice the pre-industrial level.

On the basis of known technology, the cost of meeting this goal would be high. But the track record of technological progress in other fields indicates an enormous potential for costs to fall as new ideas are developed and applied. In the energy industry, for example, the costs of deep-water oil and gas development have fallen by a factor of three over the last 15 years, dramatically extending the frontier of commercial activity . . .

Many people believe that the 500–550 ppm goal would help avoid the worst calamities. But we must recognize this assessment for what it is: a judgment informed by current knowledge, rather than a confirmed conclusion to the story . . . [T]he long-term target of 500–550 ppm is reachable even if levels of emissions continue to rise in the short term—as long as emissions start declining thereafter. (Emissions must be progressively curtailed beyond a certain point because previously emitted carbon dioxide lingers in the atmosphere for hundreds of years) . . .

Efficiency and Transformation

Both the exact level of the peak in global carbon dioxide emissions over time and the subsequent decline are unknown. We can safely assume, however, that emissions from developing countries will keep rising as economic activity and incomes grow . . . This means that leadership must come from the industrialized world.

In the short term, the developed world can use energy much more efficiently and profitably. With a clear impetus for change, business could put new technologies and services to use: cautiously at first, but more aggressively as the best systems are identified and put into practice with the normal turnover of capital.

Business has already found that it is possible to reduce emissions from its operations. Counterintuitively, BP found that it was able to reach its initial target of reducing emissions by 10 percent below its 1990 levels without cost. Indeed, the company added around $650 million of shareholder value, because the bulk of the reductions came from the elimination of leaks and waste. Other firms—such as electricity generator Entergy; car manufacturer Toyota, and mining giant Rio Tinto—are having similar experiences. The overwhelming message from these experiments is that efficiency can both pay dividends and reduce emissions.

Yet reducing emissions by . . . around 25 billion tons per year in 2050 will require more than just efficiency improvements. Given the world's rising demand for energy, we must also transform the energy system itself, making fuller use of low-carbon fuels as well as carbon-free energy systems. Paradigm shifts must occur across the economy: transportation accounts for 20 percent of total emissions, industry contributes another 20 percent, the domestic and commercial sectors emit around 25 percent, and power-generation accounts for another 35 percent. A wide-ranging set of policies is thus called for.

In power generation, options include switching from coal to less-carbon-intensive natural gas. For example, 400 new gas plants, each generating 1,000 megawatts, would reduce emissions by one billion tons per year. Such a reduction would be difficult within the parameters of today's electricity systems—400,000 megawatts is roughly equal to all of Chinas electric power capacity, or half the installed capacity in the United States. Zero-carbon fuels would also help reduce emissions. If 200,000 megawatts of coal-generated power were to be replaced with nuclear power, carbon dioxide emissions would be reduced by one billion tons per year. Progress on the nuclear front will demand investment in new technologies, as well as a viable plan for locating reactors that ensures that radioactive materials are kept out of the environment and beyond terrorists' reach.

Coal, too, could be made carbon-free, using advanced power plants that gasify the fuel and then generate power while stripping away the carbon for sequestration underground. Coal gasification could become a huge growth industry. China is among the top investors in this technology, not just because these plants are much cleaner, but also because they could be keystones in a program to synthesize clean liquid fuels for transportation needs.

More efficient buildings would also result in large energy savings, since over one-third of today's energy is used indoors. Given that electrification is a central feature of industrial and postindustrial societies, innovators must tap the potential for ultra-efficient electrical appliances. Investment in a digitally controlled power grid could aid this effort by allowing major appliances to "talk" directly with power generators so that the whole system operates closer to its optimum potential. Such a "smart grid" would reduce losses in electricity transmission while also allowing fuller use of waste heat from power generators in factories and homes.

There are efficiency savings to be made in transportation too. Given the massive advantages of gasoline over rival fuels—both in terms of its power density and its ease of storage—transport is unlikely to switch to new fuels in the near future. More promising approaches will focus on making transportation more efficient, while meeting the ever-stricter limits on other emissions that cause air pollution. For example, running 600 million diesel or gasoline cars at 60 miles per gallon (mpg) instead of 30 mpg would result in a billion fewer tons of carbon dioxide per year. Advanced ultra-efficient diesel engines, meanwhile, are so clean that even the strictest regulatory body in the world—the California Air Resources Board—is taking a second look. Advanced techniques for gasoline injection also hold promise, as do hybrid electric-gasoline cars already on the road . . .

Down to Business

The role of business is to transform possibilities into reality. And that means being practical, undertaking focused research, and testing the different possibilities in real commercial markets. The energy business is now global, which offers a tremendous advantage: international companies access knowledge around the world and apply it quickly throughout their operations.

But the business sector cannot succeed in isolation. Harnessing business potential requires fair and credible incentives to drive the process of innovation and change. In responding to global warming, that role must fall to the government. Neither prescriptive regulations nor fiscal interventions designed to collect revenue rather than to alter behavior provide the answer. Rather, governments must identify meaningful objectives and encourage the business sector to attain them by using its knowledge of technology, markets, and consumer preferences.

Recent experience suggests that emissions trading regimes—whereby government sets a binding cap on total emissions, dividing the total into "emission credits" that are given to those who emit carbon dioxide—are the best policy for encouraging business. Policymakers (notably in the United States) have demonstrated that it is possible to design such systems for other pollutants, such as sulphur dioxide, thereby harnessing the power of innovation and the flexibility of the market to protect the environment, while avoiding crippling costs. The same insights should apply to carbon dioxide. A well-designed trading regime would include a strictly enforced cap, which would make carbon dioxide emission credits scarcer (and thus more valuable) and would thereby increase the incentive for business to control emissions. Such a system would also allow firms and households the flexibility to apply resources where they have the greatest impact, which is essential, because the best measures for controlling carbon dioxide are hard to anticipate with precision and are widely dispersed across the economy. And a credible emission trading system would create incentives to invest in radical new technologies, the kind that will be crucial in building a carbon-free energy system in the future . . .

At present, the nascent European emission trading system—which [started] running on a trial basis in 2005—is the most advanced example. Built on sound monitoring and verification policies, the system is the centerpiece of the European effort to implement the commitments adopted at Kyoto. Yet there are still hurdles to be cleared if it is to be fully operational by 2008, as planned. The process for allocating emission credits is not yet complete. And the system will cover only about 40 percent of Europe's emissions as it stands—mainly those from industry. The potential for extending the scope of the trading base is indeed considerable, not least through the incorporation of effective incentives that will reward businesses whose investments reduce emissions outside Europe, such as in Russia and the emerging market economies of Asia—where large and relatively low-cost reductions of emissions are possible.

Markets are emerging in other regions as well. The Chicago Climate Exchange, opened in December 2003, involves 19 North American entities that have agreed to reduce their emissions by one percent per year over four years. Canada may yet create a market for carbon dioxide as it aims to meet the Kyoto targets. And U.S. states have become laboratories for innovation and change. For example, Massachusetts, New York, and New Hampshire are adopting rules that will spur the creation of market-based emission trading systems . . .

Offering positive incentives is one key contribution that government can make to stimulate business. Another is organizing research. It is crucial to extend our understanding of the science of climate change: monitoring key variables with sufficient precision to understand both natural variability and the climate's response to human activity. A key target of such work must be to understand the precise connection between the concentration of carbon dioxide in the atmosphere and changes in climate. Such research must also advance our knowledge of available choices: with the clock ticking, we cannot wait for definite answers before we take action.

Government intervention must take other forms too. Transforming the energy system will require new technologies with risks that will be too high (and benefits too remote) for private firms to provide all the needed investment. This is one area in which the United States, with its outstanding technical capacity, should take a leadership role . . . The priorities for such work might include photovoltaic cells (which convert sunlight into electricity), fission reactor technology, energy from biomass, and the use of hydrogen.

Given the costs and risks involved in such investment, governments with common interests and common views of the future have every incentive to combine their efforts and resources . . .

There are examples of such collaborative work already underway. In November 2003, a ministerial-level meeting held in Washington, D.C., began the process of building international partnerships for research on the potential of the hydrogen economy. The United States has already pledged $1.7 billion over the next five years for work in this area. A similar collaboration—the International Carbon Sequestration Leadership Forum—is built around the concept of capturing carbon and storing it geologically. Again, this scheme complements programs in the United States, such as FutureGen, a $1 billion public-private partnership to promote emissions-free coal fired electricity and hydrogen production. These research efforts are a good start, but they must go hand-in-hand with the creation of credible caps on emissions and trading systems, which will create the incentives to transform the energy system . . .

Unfinished Business

The appropriate response to the faltering Kyoto Protocol is neither dismay nor fatalism. A complete international agreement on a subject of such complexity and uncertainty is still a long way off. But as those who championed the cause of liberal trade found after that first meeting in 1946, great causes acquire lives of their own. Consolidated political agreements often follow, rather than lead, the realities on the ground.

Taking small steps never feels entirely satisfactory. Nor does taking action without complete scientific knowledge. But certainty and perfection have never figured prominently in the story of human progress. Business, in particular, is accustomed to making decisions in conditions of considerable uncertainty, applying its experience and skills to areas of activity where much is unknown. That is why it will have a vital role in meeting the challenge of climate change—and why the contribution it is already making is so encouraging.

TIMELINE

1979 — First World Climate Conference discusses climate change.

1985 — First international conference on the greenhouse effect takes place in Austria. Scientists discuss the various gases they believe contribute to global warming.

1987 — At the time, this is the warmest year in recorded history.

1988 — Scientists link major droughts in the United States to global warming during congressional hearings in Washington, D.C. The United Nations (UN) establishes the Intergovernmental Panel on Climate Change (IPCC) in order to analyze scientific data related to climate change.

1990 — The IPCC's first major report finds that the planet had warmed by 32.9°F (0.5°C) during the past century.

1991 — Scientists in the Philippines link a volcanic eruption and the release of its debris to a significant drop in temperature over a period of two years. Their hypothesis is that global temperatures are more volatile that they first believed.

1992 — Climate Change Convention in Rio de Janeiro drafts an agreement between fifty-four nations to reduce emissions.

1994 ——— The Alliance of Small Island States fear it will suffer from changes in sea level due to global warming. It demands a 20 percent reduction in emissions by 2005.

1995 ——— The Climate Change Convention meets in Berlin, Germany. The same year, the IPCC states that the current warming trend is "unlikely to be natural in origin." Its report suggests that humans are to blame for the rise in temperatures. If left unchecked, the report notes, global temperatures by the year 2100 are likely to rise between 33.8°F (1°C) and 38.3°F (3.5°C).

1996 ——— Second meeting of the Climate Change Convention. The United States sides with the IPCC against skeptical scientists who argue that global warming may not be a threat. Still, the effort to pursue an agreement to reduce emissions to stabilize them at 1990 levels fails.

1997 ——— The Kyoto Protocol agreement is developed to lower emissions around the world by 5.4 percent by 2010. Unfortunately, the United States refuses to ratify the agreement unless it sees "meaningful participation" in reducing emissions from developing nations.

(continued on following page)

1998 — Further negotiations to ratify the Kyoto Protocol fail, though follow-up negotiations in Buenos Aires help establish a deadline to revise the agreement by 2000.

2000 — A new report by the IPCC warns that the world could warm by as much as 42.8°F (6°C) within a century. Major flooding occurs around the world, raising concerns about extreme weather and its relationship to global warming. Again, meetings to confirm the conditions of the Kyoto Protocol fail.

2001 — President George W. Bush rejects the Kyoto Protocol because he insists that meeting its demands to reduce emissions will affect U.S. jobs and the economy. Despite this setback, other nations of the world embrace the agreement and decide to enforce it by the end of 2002.

2002 — Leaders of the European Union, Japan, and other nations of the world ratify the Kyoto Protocol, but Australia, like the United States, refuses to comply.

2003 — European nations experience the hottest summer in 300 years, leading to an estimated 30,000 deaths. Extreme weather events occur throughout the world. Russia becomes the latest nation to hesitate on whether to sign the Kyoto Protocol.

2004 —————— Russia signs the Kyoto Protocol, agreeing to begin emission reductions the following year. Scientists around the world advance research and claim that mean temperatures have already surpassed what they believe will result in catastrophe over the next century. Other scientists remain skeptical about the findings. The end of the year brings tragedy to Southeast Asian countries as a series of earthquakes become a catalyst for a massive tsunami that kills an estimated 250,000 people.

2005 —————— Dr. Rajendra Pachauri, the chairman of the IPCC, tells delegates at an international conference attended by representatives from 114 governments that he personally believes that the world has "already reached the level of dangerous concentrations of carbon dioxide in the atmosphere."

The National Science Foundation
4201 Wilson Boulevard
Arlington, VA 22230
(703) 292-5111
(800) 877-8339
Web site: http://www.nsf.gov

Pew Center on Global Climate Change
2101 Wilson Boulevard
Suite 550
Arlington, VA 22201
(703) 516-4146
Web site: http://www.pewclimate.org

US Environmental Protection Agency
1200 Pennsylvania Avenue NW (6205J)
Washington, DC 20460
(202) 343-9327
e-mail: global.warming@epa.gov
Web site: http://yosemite.epa.gov/oar/globalwarming.nsf/
content/index.html

Web Sites

Due to the changing nature of Internet links, the Rosen
Publishing Group, Inc., has developed an online list of Web
sites related to the subject of this book. This site is updated
regularly. Please use this link to access the list:

http://www.rosenlinks.com/canf/cldi

FOR FURTHER READING

Gelbspan, Ross. *Boiling Point: How Politicians, Big Oil and Coal, Journalists and Activists Have Fueled the Climate Crisis—and What We Can Do to Avert Disaster*. New York, NY: Basic Books, 2004.

Gelbspan, Ross. *The Heat Is On: The Climate Crisis, the Cover-Up, the Prescription*. Cambridge, MA: Perseus Books, 1998.

Houghton, John. *Global Warming: The Complete Briefing*. Cambridge, England: Cambridge University Press, 1998.

McKibben, Bill. *The End of Nature: Tenth Anniversary Edition*. New York, NY: Anchor Books, 1997.

Roleff, Tamara L., Scott Barbour, and Karin Swisher, eds. *Global Warming: Opposing Viewpoints*. San Diego, CA: Greenhaven Press, 1997.

Ruddiman, William E. *Plows, Plagues, and Petroleum: How Humans Took Control of Climate*. Princeton, NJ: Princeton University Press, 2005.

Spence, Chris. *Global Warming: Personal Solutions for a Healthy Planet*. New York, NY: Palgrave Macmillian, 2005.

Speth, James Gustave. *Red Sky at Morning: America and the Crisis of the Global Environment*. New Haven, CT: Yale University Press, 2004.

ANNOTATED BIBLIOGRAPHY

Abraham, Curtis. "Glacial Meltdown Threatens People Downstream." *New Scientist*, November 2, 2002), p. 44. Curtis Abraham is a staff writer for *New Scientist*. He also writes for various other publications about environmental and human rights issues. He is currently writing a book about the Ika of Uganda, Africa.
Reprinted with permission from *New Scientist*.

Alley, Richard B., et al. *Abrupt Climate Change: Inevitable Surprises*. Washington, DC: National Academies Press, 2002. Retrieved July 2005 (http://books.nap.edu/openbook/0309074347/html/index.html). Richard B. Alley is the chair of the Committee on Abrupt Climate Change for the U.S. National Academy of Science and the Professor of Geosciences and Associate Professor of the Environmental Institute College of Earth and Mineral Sciences, Pennsylvania State University.
Permission granted by The National Academies. Copyright © 2004 The National Academies.

Angelo, Claudio. "Punctuated Disequilibrium." *Scientific American*, Vol. 292, No. 2, pp. 22–23. Claudio Angelo is a science news editor of the Brazilian daily newspaper *Folha de S. Paulo*.
Reprinted with permission from Claudio Angelo.

Browne, John. "Beyond Kyoto." *Foreign Affairs*, Vol. 83, No. 4, pp. 20–32. John Browne is CEO of British Petroleum, Inc., a company considered by many to be among the most progressive in the energy market. In this article Browne contends that the private sector should set the standards for developing alternative energy standards and curbing the pace of global warming.
Reprinted by permission of *Foreign Affairs*, (July/August 2004). Copyright © (2004) by the Council on Foreign Relations, Inc.

Clark, J. R., and Dwight R. Lee. "Global Warming and Its Dangers." Independent Review, Vol. 8, No. 4, pp. 591–594. J. R. Clark is a professor of economics and occupies the Probasco Chair of Free Enterprises at the University of Tennessee, Chattanooga. Dwight R. Lee is a professor of economics and occupies the Ramsey Chair of Private Enterprise at the University of Georgia.
Sections of this article are reprinted with permission from the publisher of *The Independent Review: A Journal of Political Economy* (Spring 2004 Volume VIII, no. 4, pp. 591–594) Copyright © 2004, The Independent Institute, 100 Swan Way, Oakland, CA 94621-1428 USA; info@independent.org; http://www.independent.org

Friedmann, S. Julio and Thomas Homer-Dixon. "Out of the Energy Box." *Foreign Affairs*, Vol. 83, No. 6, pp. 72–83. S. Julio Friedmann heads the Carbon Storage Initiative at Lawrence Livermore National Laboratory. Thomas Homer-Dixon is director of the Pierre Elliott Trudeau Centre for Peace and Conflict Studies at the University of Toronto.
Reprinted by permission of *Foreign Affairs*, (November/December 2004). Copyright © (2004) by the Council on Foreign Relations, Inc.

Gelbspan, Ross. "The Heat Is On." *Harper's*, Vol. 291, No. 1747, pp. 31–37, and "Snowed." *Mother Jones*, May/June 2005. Ross Gelbspan was a reporter and editor at the *Philadelphia Bulletin*; the *Washington Post*; the *Village Voice*; and the *Boston Globe*, where he shared a Pulitzer Prize for a series he conceived and edited. He covered the UN Conference on the Environment in Stockholm in 1972, coauthored a four-part series on the occasion of the second UN conference in 1992, and addressed the World Economic Forum in Davos, Switzerland, in 1998. His work has appeared in *Harper's* and numerous other publications. He is the author of several books on global warming, including *The Heat Is On: The Climate Crisis, the Cover Up, the Prescription* (1998) and

Boiling Point: How Politicians, Big Oil and Coal, Journalists and Activists Have Fueled The Climate Crisis—and What We Can Do to Avert Disaster (2004). Gelbspan's Web site (http://www.heatisonline.org) was rated the best climate-related site by the Pacific Institute.

Halweil, Brian. "The Irony of Climate." *WorldWatch*, Vol. 18, No. 2, 2005, pp. 18–23. Brian Halweil graduated from Stanford University with a degree in earth systems and biology. He has been a senior researcher at WorldWatch Institute since 1997. He has written for the *New York Times*, the *Los Angeles Times*, and the *Washington Post*. Halweil was recently invited to testify before the U.S. Senate on the role of biotechnology in combating hunger in developing nations. He is also the author of *Eat Here: Reclaiming Homegrown Pleasures in a Global Supermarket* (2004).

Houghton, John. *Global Warming: The Complete Briefing*. Cambridge, England: Cambridge University Press, 1994. John Houghton is cochair of the Scientific Assessment Working Group of the Intergovernmental Panel on Climate Change (IPCC) and was formerly chief executive of the Meteorological Office in Great Britain.

Jensen, Mari N. "Climate Warming Shakes Up Species," *BioScience*, Vol. 54, No. 8, pp. 722–729. Mari N. Jensen is a freelance writer who specializes in environmental issues. Her articles have appeared in many scientific publications

including *Science News* and on the Internet at Web sites
such as ABC News and WebMD.
Bioscience by Jensen. Copyright © 2004 by American Institute of Biological
Sciences. Reproduced with permission of American Institute of Biological
Sciences in the format Other Book, via Copyright Clearance Center.

Meserve, Richard A. "Global Warming and Nuclear Power."
Science, Vol. 303, No. 5657, p. 433. Richard A. Meserve
was chairman of the U.S. Nuclear Regulatory
Commission (NRC) from 1999 to 2003. Before joining
the NRC, Meserve was a partner in the Washington,
D.C., firm of Covington & Burling. With his 1975
Harvard law degree and his 1976 Ph.D. in applied
physics from Stanford, he devoted his legal practice to
technical issues arising in environmental and toxic tort
litigation, counseling scientific societies and high-tech
companies, and nuclear licensing. Meserve serves on the
Board of Directors of the American Association for the
Advancement of Science.
Reprinted with permission from "Global Warming and Nuclear Power," by
Richard A. Meserve, *Science* 303:433 (2004). Copyright © 2004 AAAS.

Pearce, Fred. "Climate Change: Menace or Myth?" *New
Scientist*, February 12, 2005, pp. 38–43. Fred Pearce is
an environment writer and frequent contributor to scien-
tific journals and is the environment consultant to *New
Scientist* magazine. His books include *Deep Jungle*
(2005), *Keepers of the Spring* (2004), and *When the
Rivers Run Dry* (2005).
Reprinted with permission from *New Scientist*.

Revkin, Andrew C. "Eskimos Seek to Recast Global Warming
as a Rights Issue." *New York Times*, December 15, 2004
and "Global Warming Is Expected to Raise Hurricane
Intensity." *New York Times*, September 30, 2004. Andrew
C. Revkin is the environment reporter for the *New York*

Times. He writes about the issues surrounding global warming and climate disruption around the world.

Ruddiman, William E. "How Did Humans First Alter Global Climate?" *Scientific American*, Vol. 292, No. 3, pp. 46–53. In this controversial article, Ruddiman, professor emeritus of environmental sciences at the University of Virginia, discusses his theories about how man's first attempts at agriculture helped raise CO_2 levels, affecting global warming. Ruddiman is also the author of *Earth's Climate: Past and Future* (2000), and *Plows, Plagues, and Petroleum: How Humans Took Control of Climate* (2005). He has published articles in *Scientific American*, *Nature*, and *Science* as well as various other scientific journals.

Stipp, David. "The Pentagon's Weather Nightmare." *Fortune*, Vol. 149, No. 3, p. 100. David Stripp is the science and environmental writer for *Fortune* magazine.

INDEX

A

agriculture/crops
    crop yields, 76, 77–88, 93
    local crops, 85–88, 160
    rice cultivation/irrigation,
        36, 43
agroforestry, 83–84
Allen, Hartwell, 79–80
American Meteorological
        Society, 6
American Petroleum Institute, 17
Arctic Climate Impact
        Assessment Group, 6
Arctic snowmelts, 5–6, 16, 107,
        148, 149
Artaxo, Paulo, 59–60

B

Baker, D. James, 123
Balling, Robert, 17, 18, 19, 122
Beever, Erik, 61, 67
Bellamy, David, 117
Bender, Marty, 86, 87, 88
bioclimatic envelope
        modeling, 69–72
Browne, Lord, 92
Burson-Marsteller, 17

C

Calder, Nigel, 119
carbon dioxide (CO$_2$)
    causes of increase in, 109, 159
    effects of, 59, 79–80, 93, 95,
        109, 114
    levels of, 36, 37–38, 39,
        41–42, 43, 44, 45, 92,
        95–96, 111, 112, 113,
        115, 131, 144, 159

carbon sequestration, 89–90, 92,
        94, 100–106, 164
coal, 96, 99, 122, 163, 164
Collins, David, 57
Comer, Gary, 149
corporate conflicts of interest,
        12–13, 16–17, 19–20,
        117, 121, 122–123
Crichton, Michael, 7, 108

D

deforestation, 36, 38, 43–44, 58,
        59, 159
Dias, Maria Assunção da Silva,
        59–60
droughts, 29, 30, 34, 60, 80, 81,
        93, 127

E

Ebell, Myron, 116
El Niño, 26, 30, 78
Elsner, James B., 75
Emanuel, Kerry A., 74, 75
energy
    consumption of, 93–96,
        162–165
    sources of, 88–92
Environmental Defense Fund, 17
Epps, Clinton W., 68

F

Fitter, Alastair, 64
Fitter, Richard, 64
floods/flooding, 29, 30, 34, 50, 51,
        57, 73, 74, 81, 128, 160
fossil fuels, 94, 100, 103, 116, 123
Francou, Bernard, 56
Friis-Christensen, Eigil, 118

About the Editor

Robert Chehoski is a film archivist, writer, and environmental activist. He is an educator in various groups that help inform people about energy conservation and methods by which they can become more environmentally conscious. He is a frequent rider with Critical Mass, a global movement of cyclists whose goal is to increase awareness about eco-friendly transportation alternatives. Chehoski lives in San Francisco, where he makes every effort to reduce pollution by riding his bike and eating locally grown foods.

Photo Credits

Cover © Paul Hardy/Corbis.

Designer: Gene Mollica; Editor: Joann Jovinelly